I Never Heard My Father Sing
And Other Memories

Gus H. Jacob

This book recounts events and reflections of Gus H. Jacob, according to the author's recollection and from the author's perspective. The events and experiences detailed herein have been faithfully rendered as remembered by the author, to the best of his ability, or as told to the author by others.

In some cases names have been changed and duly noted in the narratives in which they appear.

TO THE MEMORY OF MY PARENTS

GUS and AMANDA JACOB

Front Cover Photograph - Malachi Talbott

Back Cover Sketch - Noah Harris

Layout - Pamela Mintari

Sketches - Abigail Harris
          Bridget Harris
          Noah Harris
          Zachary Harris
          Arleah Talbott

Proofreading / Critique - Camille Harris
                          Gabrielle Harris
                          Pamela Mintari
                          Lorraine Talbott

Historical Photographs -   Evangeline Daniell
                            John Jacob
                            Camille Harris
                            Author's collection

If you don't know where you're from...
You can't know who you are

Unknown

CONTENTS

GROWING UP

HIGH SCHOOL-COLLEGE-BEYOND

PERSONAL MUSINGS

PREFACE

Every generation has a story to tell, but many go untold. Far too often memories fade and treasured recollections are lost. Beyond the public documentaries of historical events lie the stories of personal family experiences. My own family is no exception. It has a rich heritage, both cultural and spiritual. Thankfully, a few letters and records remain but so much is missing. How I wish I knew the details - the routine events of their lives and how they reacted in particular situations. If only I had taken the time to talk with them. What was it like growing up in the early part of the twentieth century? What moments did they celebrate? How did they confront challenges, disappointments and heartaches?

In the mid 1990's I began writing the "stories" that follow. The idea was simply to relate personal thoughts, experiences and memories for my children and grandchildren. Originally, I called the endeavor "Musings and Memories" – Musings, in that I might share a few personal thoughts for my progeny – and memories, well, that's what most of it is – memories of my life – particularly my childhood and youth.

I have given up the attempt to present these narratives in precise chronological order. They never originated "on paper" in that way. Most were written as they came to mind or if someone might say to me, "Remember when we....". At times I would write at length, then lay my "pen" aside for a while – even years. I realize that I might, in some cases, repeat myself. Circumstances and chronology may not agree from one writing to the next, although in editing the entire project I have tried to unscramble any inconsistencies.

The middle of the 20th Century was a unique time in history. In several instances I have used terms or syntax common to the time, although, in the 21st Century they might not be considered appropriate or politically correct. No offense is intended, only an attempt to present the reality of my experiences and of the culture common to the time and place.

I trust that this collection will help present a glimpse of life in an era that came and went and is no more. Some items may only be of interest to my family (which was the original intent of the project). To those who may find little interest in some selections, I ask your indulgence of my personal divergences.

*** *** ***

...as for us, our days are like grass; it flourishes like a flower in the field; the wind blows over it, and it's gone; even its place remembers it no more

Psalm 103:15, 16

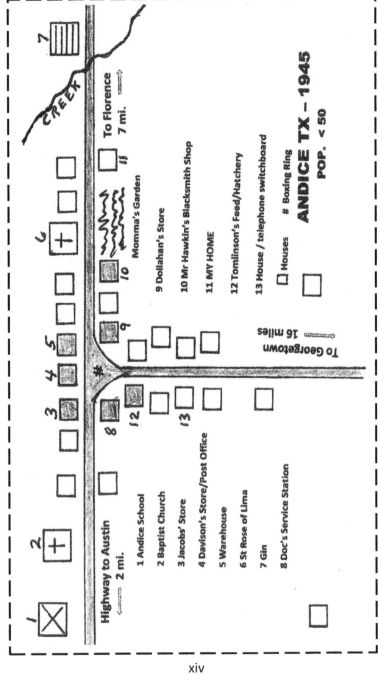

ANDICE TX – 1945
POP. < 50

1 Andice School
2 Baptist Church
3 Jacobs' Store
4 Davison's Store/Post Office
5 Warehouse
6 St Rose of Lima
7 Gin
8 Doc's Service Station
9 Dollahan's Store
10 Mr Hawkin's Blacksmith Shop
11 MY HOME
12 Tomlinson's Feed/Hatchery
13 House / telephone switchboard

☐ Houses   # Boxing Ring

Momma's Garden

Highway to Austin
2 mi.

To Florence
7 mi.

To Georgetown
16 miles

CREEK

xiv

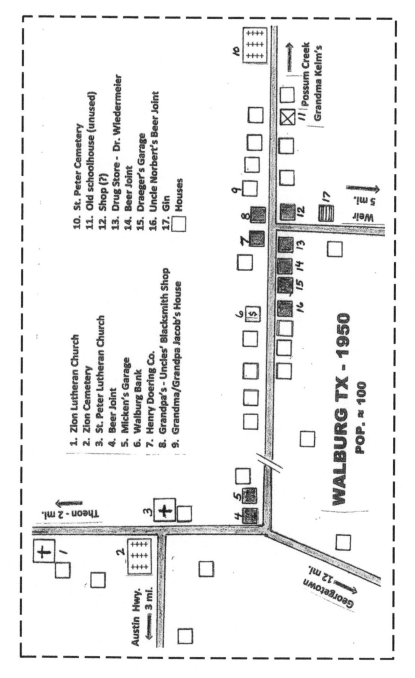

1. Zion Lutheran Church
2. Zion Cemetery
3. St. Peter Lutheran Church
4. Beer Joint
5. Micken's Garage
6. Walburg Bank
7. Henry Doering Co.
8. Grandpa's - Uncles' Blacksmith Shop
9. Grandma/Grandpa Jacob's House

10. St. Peter Cemetery
11. Old schoolhouse (unused)
12. Shop (?)
13. Drug Store - Dr. Wiedermeier
14. Beer Joint
15. Draeger's Garage
16. Uncle Norbert's Beer Joint
17. Gin
☐ Houses

WALBURG TX - 1950
POP. ≈ 100

Theon - 2 mi.
Austin Hwy. — 3 mi.
Georgetown ⟵ 12 mi.
Weir 5 mi.
Possum Creek
Grandma Kelm's

Gus Henry Jacob - Age 3

GROWING UP

Age 12

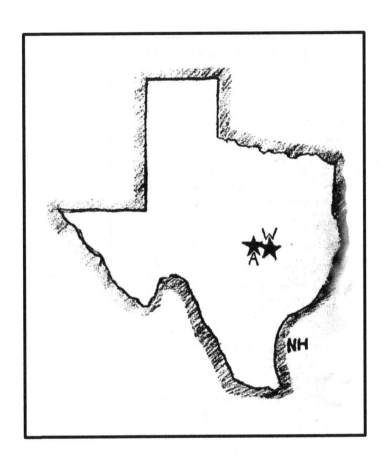

MY TWO HOMETOWNS

ANDICE - a funny cognomination for a town.

A fter the Civil War a small group of families settled along a nameless Central Texas stream now known as Berry's Creek. The community was then called by several unofficial names. In the early 1890's Isaac Newton (no relation to the English scientist) and his wife moved to the area.

Their son AUDICE was born in 1899 and shortly thereafter Newton applied for a post office, requesting it be named after his son. A Washington bureaucrat misread the application and approved the post office as ANDICE.[1] And it's been Andice ever since.

The town I knew as a boy was not unlike thousands of other rural settlements in America in the mid-20th century - if one dares to call it a town. It wasn't on the map - just a spot where two country roads met to form a "T". The nearest paved highway was two miles west of town, a quick, smooth forty mile trek to Austin. Driving south, down the leg of the "T", the road to Georgetown was over fifteen miles of mud when it rained or ruts and dust when it didn't. With ten times the population of Andice, Florence lay seven equally grimy miles to the east.

---

[1] *History of Andice & Community 1851-1987,* Harold B. Asher, (unpublished)

As I was growing up, Andice had hardly more than forty to fifty residents at any given time, although I'm told that in the 1920's it was home for over a hundred. It then boasted a drug store, barber shop, "picture show," (movies Friday & Saturday nights only) and a hotel. By 1940 most of the ancillary structures had been torn down, moved or converted into small homes. The leg of the T became aptly dubbed as "Widder Lane," considering the number of homes occupied by husbandless ladies.

Several businesses clustered around the intersection. Daddy and Uncle Ben owned one of the three grocery stores. Directly across the road was Doc Davis' service station (two pumps and a mechanic's bay). Tomlinson's Feed Store stood next to Doc's garage, and Dollahan's Grocery crowded the opposite corner. In a single two-room structure a one-chair barber shop, and a third small grocery run by Miz Davidson flanked our families' store.

Our house, along with several others, was east of "downtown." Momma's garden paralleled the road and at the far end of the vegetable rows Mr. Hawkins' labored in the combination blacksmith shop and gristmill. Across the road sat the Catholic church, and at the eastern edge of town, just on the other side of the creek, Mr. McCann managed the cotton gin.

West of the "T-junction" were several other houses, the Baptist church, a four-classroom public school and finally the community cemetery. The only "business" on Widder Lane was the telephone switchboard in Mrs. Windsor's home

Near the intersection, the leg of the T broadened to create a large open space where vehicles of all sorts would haphazardly park, allowing room for traffic to squeeze by. For a while a light pole and a platform for boxing matches or local musicians occupied the middle of this intersectory space. Four posts and a single rope defined the ring where local toughs could settle scores or establish bragging rights. I don't know which the crowd enjoyed most, the pugilistic performances or the occasional duet of an old time fiddle and banjo on a hot Saturday night.

A single-bulb light on the pole at one corner of the ring lit the small, makeshift plaza. Farmers and their families, in town on Saturday afternoons for the necessities of the coming week, would linger to gossip, discuss the weather, crops and cattle - then stay for the entertainment. As the evening wore on, the music ended, the excitement died - everyone headed home. The last one to leave town would turn off the light.

*** *** ***

Daddy came to Andice sometime around 1930, before he and Momma were married. He had come to work as a clerk in the cotton gin owned by his uncle, Charlie. Cotton was the main cash crop of the time. After picking, it had to be seeded and baled. The picked cotton, hauled by horse or mule-drawn wagons, headed to the nearest gin. Uncle Charlie owned five gins scattered throughout the county, most in communities that primarily spoke German or Czech.

The Andice gin was Charlie Doering's most remote operation. Although German was Daddy's mother-tongue, he understood and spoke English as well, and with only eight years of formal education, he was admitted to and subsequently earned a diploma from a business school in Waco. The bookkeeping training and a command of the language made Daddy the prime candidate to oversee his uncle's interests in the English-only community of Andice.

His few years at the gin gave Daddy the experience needed to grade, buy, and sell cotton as a broker: After the cotton was "ginned" and wrapped in 500 pound bales, a sample, the size of a small loaf of bread, was cut from each bale. Bale and sample were tagged with an identical lot numbers. Daddy would examine the sample, grade it for quality, and offer a price for the bale. The sample was forwarded to a buyer in Houston or Galveston who would repeat the process and make Daddy an offer. In the meantime, Daddy's bales remained in the gin yard or the vacant lot near our house.

Daddy didn't become rich, but his earnings did assist in financing his venture into the grocery and mercantile business. In late summer the shelves near the rear of the store bulged with bundles of ginned samples, as Daddy continued to broker cotton until the gin ceased operation sometime in the '50's.

*** *** ***

WALBURG - German and Lutheran to the core

After 1850 the State of Texas experienced a large influx of European emigrants – Germans, Czechs, Wends – most settling in a broad stretch of central Texas. Daddy's maternal grand-father, Henry Doering was among the multitude. He planted his roots some 10 miles north of Georgetown. Others followed. The community that emerged became WALBURG, named after Henry's hometown in Germany. He established a bank and operated the largest mercantile and general store for miles around. For more than a hundred years the enterprise was family-owned and managed. Today the bank building stands empty, closed by larger financial interests. But the mercantile building is still in use – now a popular German restaurant - and faded lettering on its façade still identifies the proud heritage of The Henry Doering Company.

Daddy had undoubtedly acquired much of his business acumen from his father and grandfather. His papa, my grandpa, Henry Jacob, was Walburg's village blacksmith, a craftsman valuable to any rural community in those days. Living in America, but serving both German and Slovak farmers, required that he communicate in three languages. Most were cash transactions, but barter was not out of the question, and Grandpa was quite resourceful in turning bartered payment into liquid assets.

*** *** ***

Momma grew up a few miles east of Walburg. She and Daddy had known each other all of their lives – attended the same school and worshipped (in German, of course) every Sunday in the same church. While Daddy was raised in town, Momma was a farm girl - the third of six children in her family and the second of five girls. In the late 1920's she too left home, but not for additional schooling. Her venture was to the big and distant city of Austin, where she served as a nanny and live-in maid. She never said much about that experience. There may have been some incidences that she just wouldn't, or couldn't, share.

*** *** ***

I know nothing about my parent's courtship. But in 1932, at the height of the Great Depression, they married and made Andice their home. Daddy had left his work at the gin and opened his first 'store,' renting space in the Tomlinson Feed Store. However, by the time I was born, he and Uncle Ben were partners and had erected a new, larger building which served them for the remainder of their business careers.

In 1934, my sister, Evangeline ("Vangie") was born. I arrived in January of '39, about three years before the Japanese attacked Pearl Harbor. Adolph Hitler was menacing Europe, and the rumblings of war were an ominous reality to Americans once again. Sister, Arlene, came along in 1944, and brother, John completed the family in 1950.

8

In the 21st century it is difficult to imagine the effect that distance had in the first half of the 20th century. The twenty miles between Andice and Walburg was far more than just a 30 to 40 minute drive by car. It was a communication barrier as well. Only a few homes had telephones; transmission quality was poor, and long-distance charges were expensive. A one-hour phone visit with an out-of-town friend was simply out of the question.

Traveling country roads in those days was slow, irritating and uncomfortable. Automobile air-conditioning wasn't even heard of. Drive with the windows rolled down and dust from passing cars engulfs everyone. Slow down for any reason with the wind at your back and your own dirt storm catches up with you.

Everyone avoided traveling in heavy rains, unless it was to church or a dire emergency. Always the risk of getting stuck in the mud or slipping off the road with the unlikely probability of another car passing soon. Add the discomfort of riding in a closed vehicle on a hot day – windows rolled up – mud from a passing truck spattering the windshield (and no windshield washers either).

*** *** ***

Before World War II thousands of hamlets, not unlike Andice, were scattered all over the United States. Most people lived and worked on farms. Roads were unpaved. Farming families ventured to the "city" less than once a month. In the meantime, all they needed could be found a few miles down a rutted road to places like Andice.

But hope was on the horizon. In the early "50's" paved roads began to appear in rural areas. No longer a muddy or dusty trek, but smooth sailing, not only into Andice for gossip and groceries but Georgetown and Austin were now comfortable drives away. And with the advent of modern roads came the decline of the small towns. The little grocery next to Daddy's had already closed and boarded up. Only two remained. In larger towns cheaper gasoline was accessible and business dropped at Doc Davis' gas station. I maintain that it was only the personal service and my father's smiling personality that kept Jacob's Store alive.

To go to church or not was never a topic of discussion in our home. Sunday worship was assumed. It was as natural as breathing. Walburg was home for both Momma and Daddy as well as grandmas, grandpas, aunts, uncles, brothers, sisters, cousins. And Sunday was more than worship. For six days the only faces many farm folk saw were those across the table and the one in the mirror. Thus, in addition to worship and praise, Sunday was for visitin' – standing 'round the huge oak outside church or sitting 'round Grandma's table. Sunday made the rest of the week meaningful and purposeful for everyone. Be it Sunday, Thanksgiving, or Christmas – you name it, in our home, church came first, invariably followed by feasting with one relative or another and an entire afternoon with cousins. After supper, the skies already dark, we headed back.

One could say that we had two hometowns.

Walburg - our spiritual hometown - a weekly destination for worship and renewal of emotional ties knotted into our ethnic identity and extended family.

Andice - our physical hometown, where, day by day, we lived and worked and played - and where each night we rested our heads and hearts in peace - not even bothering to lock our doors.

Home Sweet Home

BIMM BOMM

*B*imm Bomm was my 'baby talk' word for Zion Lutheran Church's bell-towered edifice and has always been associated with one of my earliest memories of childhood: our family motoring the twenty-some miles to worship on Sunday mornings.

> *I am not yet two years old. The '39 Chevy is nearing the end of the half-hour trip - sister, Vangie, in the seat behind - me, standing on the front seat between Daddy and Momma as we climb a low rise on the dusty road. Zion Church and its prominent steeple leap into view. "Bimm-bomm," I shout, pointing toward the top of the hill beyond. For me, the term for the old, tall wooden structure and all it entailed was synonymous with the tone of its two massive bells. "Yes, bimm-bomm,"Momma replies, "we're almost there."*

As I grew older, "bimm-bomm" became relegated to the recesses of my mind as infantile vocabulary – but the weighty bells continued to be a source of wonder and awe.

Inside the church, squirms a fidgety youngster, weary at the thought of the worship soon to begin - German liturgy, songs and sermon - all beyond his interest or comprehension.

> *I turn in the pew and focus on the rear balcony. Far above, two rough ropes hang side by side through holes in the lofty ceiling to the floor below. Reaching high as he*

13

can, an usher firmly grips each and struggles to waken the sleeping giants. At   first - no sound at all. But as his vantage on the cords   lengthens, the chiming begins - alternately, a deep descending musical "fourth"– "BIMM – BOMM --- BIMM – BOMM ---- BIMM – BOMM." The "baby talk" echoes in my head. With each peal the bell ringer bobs up and down. Once in motion, the bells sway almost effortlessly under \their own weight. But, my eyes are fixed as the mighty belfry pair lifts their master from the floor as he clings to the ropes, ala Quasimodo. The ringing continues. Then, with a heavy strain he heaves back on both lines at once – reigning in the team of "headstrong horses" - and the sound fades to echo in the distance.
"What fun that must be!" I marvel.

Through the years I had always believed that "bimm – bomm" was nothing more than baby-talk, unique to my immediate family. I don't recall ever hearing it used by any of my relatives. I was sure that my mother made it up - just for me.

My "bubble" burst several years ago. An outdoor Christmas concert televised from The Netherlands closed with a song about the town's bells. All over the courtyard the crowd joined in the lieder. "Bimm – bomm ….. bimm – bomm" they sang. I couldn't believe my ears! "Bimm - bomm" had always been mine alone. What a wonderful disappointment to discover "Bimm -bomm" isn't just an infant's babbling - it's a cherished onomatopoeia sung 'round the world!

AUNT OLGA'S SCARECROW

U nbelievable! During WWII there were over 500 stockades in the United States, housing almost a half-million German, Italian, and Japanese prisoners of war. One such was at Camp Hood (now Fort Hood) only twenty-five miles, as the crow flies, from Andice.

We had received word that two German prisoners escaped and were probably making their way to Mexico, a neutral nation. Since we lived along a direct line to the Rio Grande, we were warned to be constantly alert, especially at night - the runaways would most likely hide during the day and travel under the cover of darkness, living off of whatever they might steal for their two-hundred mile trip. Anything to assist them along the way - any form of transportation to speed their journey along, particularly unlocked vehicles and fuel from farm storage tanks. An automobile might be faster, but two farm hands on a tractor, driving south on a country road, wouldn't raise an eyebrow.

Housewives were advised not to leave their washing on the line after it had dried. If the two could obtain new clothes for their prison uniforms, they might even risk hitchhiking, since they both spoke English. Farmhouse wives were understandably fearful - during the day they would be alone with the children, while husbands tended crops or were otherwise absent.

Panic began to spread when one mother found her fresh-baked apple pie missing from the back porch where she had placed it to cool. A quick phone call and the word went out. Party lines came alive. The rumor continued long after the missing dessert was found. It had never made it to the porch after all. She had quickly set the pie aside on a shelf near the stairs and rushed up to referee a battle between two rowdy youngsters.

My aunt wasn't taking any chances. Although Uncle Ben was young, athletic and strong, no one was going to convince him to stand guard outside - not even one night. But Aunt Olga was resourceful. She would find a way: something to dissuade the approach of the dangerous POW's in the dark. By nightfall, with a large broomstick in hand, a six-foot, straw-stuffed scarecrow boldly guarded the front lawn of the Ben Jacob estate.

The dreaded fugitives were eventually apprehended in the cedar brakes near Austin. They had travelled less than seventy miles in eight days. However, in case the report of their capture had only been a hopeful rumor, Sergeant Scarecrow remained at his post until the good news was verified in the Austin papers. The courageous sentinel was then discharged, undressed, un-stuffed and Uncle Ben reclaimed his floppy hat, red plaid shirt and a favorite pair of overalls.

LOST IN AUSTIN

Shopping in Austin was a semi-annual ritual for Momma – springtime before Easter and each autumn as Christmas drew near. Sometimes Daddy accompanied her to town but left her to shop alone, while he found business to address or watch the stock market "board" at the local office of *Merrill, Lynch, Pierce, Fenner & Beane.*

I was five, going on six that December, as I followed behind Momma through the Christmas crowd as she wheeled baby sister, Arlene, in her pram. Once in a while she would take my hand, but most of the time she relied on me to just keep my eye on the carriage and toddle along.

In 1944 enclosed malls were far in the future. The sidewalks on both sides of Congress Avenue were streaming with shoppers. Every yuletide *Scarborough's*, Austin's most fashionable department store, decorated its large display windows with fanciful Christmas scenes. In one, mechanical elves toiled in a workshop, creating the toys to be found inside. In the next window, elves in a park hoisted drinking mugs as a full stream of pink lemonade flowed into a birdbath from a huge faucet floating in mid-air - impossible! There was no other plumbing attached. Wide-eyed youngsters stood open-mouthed and craned their necks for a better look at the magic. I pushed my way through the crowd to join them.

"Come on, Gus Henry!" (Everyone called me by both names). "Come on," Momma called, "We still have to get you some shoes at *Buster Brown's*, and its three blocks away!"

She didn't realize that three blocks is three miles for a foot-sore five-year-old who would rather be at the toy department at *Scarborough's?* Just follow the carriage ...follow the carriage... hold Momma's hand... cross the street....push past bellies...don't bump into backsides ...follow the carriage...

*** *** ***

I didn't say it, but my mind screamed: "HEY! YOU'RE NOT MY MOMMA! ...AND WHAT ARE YOU DOING WITH MY BABY SISTER?" It wasn't Momma – just a strange woman pushing a pram that looked a lot like the one Arlene was in. "WHERE'S MY MOMMA?" I cried aloud. Through a wall of tears appeared a kind face with a gentle voice. "Don't cry, little boy. We'll find your momma." she assured me.

*** *** ***

There I was, sitting in a room surrounded by blue uniforms handing me do-nuts, hot chocolate, and a pair of real handcuffs. One policeman tried to arrest Jo-Gee-Jo, my stuffed elephant friend, but before he got the chance I manacled the officer to a chair with his own handcuffs – *he wasn't going anywhere!* And no one was taking Jo-Gee-Jo!

The tears had stopped and I was no longer thinking about Momma when a familiar face came through the door. Daddy wasn't smiling… but he wasn't angry either.

Was that a tear rolling down his cheek?

SCHOOL DAZE

The aging "T-shaped" red-brick school-house still stands at the edge of town, a not-to-be-ignored reminder of days long gone. Shouts and laughter of children no longer echo in its hallways. Weary teachers no longer relish the silence of empty rooms at the end of a hectic day. Grinning parents no longer swell with pride as their darlings, decked in red and white "rhythm band" uniforms, rap sticks, tinkle triangles, crash cymbals, and click castanets, filling the 200 seat auditorium with rhythmic noise - music to their mothers' ears.

Now, the old, dying structure struggles to serve as a community center and venue for reunions and receptions. But that, too, is destined to fade, as modern air-conditioned activity halls of nearby churches prove far more comfortable and convenient.

Constructed in the 1920's, it originally housed classes through high school. The dusty, dirt roads, stretching in three directions from the middle of town, funneled students from miles around. By the time I enrolled in 1945, the four upper grades had been transferred to the high school in Florence, seven miles away. Now, with several rooms used for storage, four remained for instruction – grades one to eight – two grades per room - plus an office and an auditorium.

The only plumbing on the 5-acre site was a multi-spigot water fountain in front of the building. Two outhouses – one for boys, one for girls – were strategically placed far to the rear and a safe distance from each other. The playground for the lower grades had a three-unit see-saw; a sturdy high, metal slide; wooden-seated swings; an open merry-go-round and a "giant stride" centrifugal swing - all far too dangerous for any playground today. On the opposite side were the softball field and a packed-dirt basketball court with wood plank backboards and net-less rims. A volleyball court lay somewhere in between.

*** *** ***

September 2, 1945 – Japan surrenders – WWII is finally over. Hitler is dead. Germany had surrendered several months earlier.

*** *** ***

September 10, 1945 - school begins.

The school year never started before Labor Day. Crops were still being harvested and any number of kids would arrive for the first day, register and not return until the last of the cotton had been picked. But that didn't affect me, a "town-kid." I was six – my first day of school – no kindergarten or pre-school in those days.

The room was huge! Five rows of desks anchored in tandem to wooden slats – seven or eight desks to the row – enough to accommodate both grades one and two. Single-bulb, globed light fixtures hung from its pressed-tin ceiling some twelve feet above. Year after year the unfinished wooden floor had been swept each day with oiled sawdust. The petroleum smell and the reminiscence of hundreds of children who had faced Miz Stapp thru the years still lingered. On one wall a bank of large windows breathed in the cool morning air, giving an element of freshness to the building, but that would change as the day went on. September weather in Central Texas is hot. Add the sweaty bodies of thirty kids, most only bathed on Saturday nights (if even then)..... I'll leave the rest to your imagination.

On a slightly raised dais Miz Stapp stood behind her desk in front of one blackboard. (Married or not, the lady teachers were addressed as Miss or more phonetically "Miz") She was a nice lady with a pleasant smile.

"Now, Gus Henry, you come, take your seat here on the first row, right behind your cousin, Katherine Anne, OK?" she smiled, "You brought your cigar box? - pencil? - crayons? scissors? paste?"

"Yes ma'am."
"And your Big Chief tablet?"
"Yes ma'am, right here!" I slid into place, carefully lifted my desk top and put everything away.

*** *** ***

It was a time and culture when many of us were called by both our given names. My best friend in town (my only friend in town) was Marshall Craig – his older brother was Bennie Baine. But it was not the case for the Stark

27

brothers who lived on a nearby farm. There were so many of them I suppose it took too much time to call them all together by both names. There were several older brothers and then Clarence and Milton and little brother, Weldon, whom I guess you might say had two names – we called him "Pee Wee" but his family called him "Babe."

There were a couple of older boys in town, and as far as I was concerned they all had the same name: TROUBLE. If they were around I wanted to be somewhere else. – they scared me spit-less – I walked on the opposite side of the road if I could and never rode my bike in front of their house. "Kraut" - "Square-head" – "Nazi" that's what they called me. I didn't understand it then, but a "German" kid in an all-American community was a frequent, and "justifiable" target in a time when fathers and brothers had been fighting a moustached madman in Europe. Though the war was over, emotions still ran deep. Thankfully, the years have healed the wounds, and the animosities between all of us have long been forgiven and forgotten.

*** *** ***

"Now, all of you place your lunches on the shelf in the back of the room," Miz Stapp instructed. "Then take your seats for a few minutes before we all go to assembly."

What's assembly? Guess we'll soon find out. I lifted my lunch box to the shelf. It was shiny, black – brand new – with a rounded lid that held a real thermos. It's only defect was where my mother had taken an ice-pick and crudely scratched "Gus Henry" on one side-panel. "You don't want to get it mixed up with Katherine Anne's," my mother had insisted. "She has one exactly like yours." I turned the damaged side to the wall. Several others completed the collection of store-bought lunch kits. Emptied half-gallon molasses pails with wire handles were lunch buckets for some - brown paper bags also served the purpose. A couple of "Meskin" kids brought nothing at all. I returned to my seat and waited.

Miz Stapp continued, "First of all, I want to give you some instructions. If you wish to ask a question raise your hand with all five fingers showing.... like this," she demonstrated. "However, if you need to go to the outhouse hold up either one finger or two fingers. You know what that means?"

"Yes, ma'am," we all chimed in unison. In the mornings there were usually several hands with a single extended digit. However, not long after lunch the 'atmosphere' in the room signaled that the "twos" would soon be held aloft.

A hand-bell rang out at the other end of the building. Doors opened and kids were stirring and shuffling. "Time for assembly," Miz Stapp declared. "Everyone, line up, single file – that means one behind the other," she explained, " – first grade, first - second grade last.......You second-graders! ...you know what to do. Help out the young-uns.....Now follow me..... and NO TALKING!!" she warned, wagging her long index finger. She meant business!

It turned out that 'assembly' was just a get-together of all the kids, the teachers, and at times some parents and visitors. Everyone marched into the auditorium - first-graders on the front row – the second graders next, etc. The big kids sat in the rows behind.

The principal, tall and somber, clopped down the aisle and took the stage. Forcing a grin, he welcomed everyone. "Glad to see so many smiling faces!" *(A lie. I doubt that he was glad and, except for us dumb first-graders few others were smiling).* He introduced the new teacher for grades three and four and promised her she would come to "just love little Andice," *(another lie),* and ...."blah ...blah...blah." Thankful that the war was over, we sang *God Bless Our Native Land,* said the *Pledge of Allegiance* the Baptist preacher had a prayer....and that was 'assembly.'

If the teachers needed to meet alone, a few ladies they called 'room mothers,' conducted 'assembly.' One played the piano while another directed the singing, waving her hands like a song-leader at a tent-meeting revival. There was *Old McDonald Had a Farm* for the smaller kids, since they couldn't read the song books. If you didn't know the words, you could just hum along. We sang Negro songs like *Go Down Moses* and *Old Black Joe* – hymns: *Onward Christian Soldiers - What a Friend We Have in Jesus* - And, of course, a few patriotic songs: *Battle Hymn of the Republic - America the Beautiful,* and the like. I knew most of them by heart before I ever started school. (I've been told that at the age of two I sang *God Bless America* solo at some function in the auditorium. But I don't remember that.)

Back in the classroom, studies continued, Miz Stapp alternated her attention between the new crop of first graders and the returning seconds. And to my delight, before sending us home she handed out our first "reader," – *Look and See* from the popular "Dick and Jane" series. I had learned to read before starting school, and I drank-in the entire book - all 50 pages or so - as soon as I got home. The next morning, however, what a disappointment to learn that I couldn't exchange it for another! I had to plod through it all again with the rest of the class, several pages each day - page one: *Oh, oh, oh* – page two: *Look, look, look* - page three: *Look, look, oh look.* After what seemed like an eternity we finally came to the end, having read and re-read less than half-dozen different words in a seemingly endless myriad of short sentences and phrases. Finally! Something new at last – the next in the series ... p.1 *See Spot*...p.2 *See Spot Run*....p3 *Run, run, run* ....(sigh).......

*** *** ***

No phonics – no new math – no 'common core' - two or more grade levels in a single room of forty kids, it's a wonder civilization survived, having had such educational disadvantages in backwoods schools around the nation. Surprising, isn't it? Those 'under-privileged' students eventually gave us radio, television, atomic energy, jet aircraft, satellites in space, cell phones, computers, etc., etc., etc.

Unfortunately, however, there is another very effective instrument of instruction that has long since disappeared – the ubiquitous *"board of education."* It came in various and sundry forms: a smooth wooden plank standing in the corner of the room – a worn leather strap on a hook behind a door – or, as in Miz Stapp's class, a slender willow branch in plain and constant view on the top of her desk.

A willow 'twig' presented a real and constant threat to most of us. If it ever found her nimble hand, with her steely-eyed glare as she slapped it against her thigh, it stirred visions of the additional dire consequences awaiting at home - enough to quickly alter the behavior and demeanor of a six-year-old boy.

*** *** ***

Eventually, those absent from school for farm work would drift back to the classroom. Larger desks had to be provided for anyone too big for the standard desks of a particular grade level. This was especially true of some of the Meskin boys. I'll always remember Lupe. He sat at a larger desk at the back of the room – a second-grader – quiet and sullen. Someone said he was sixteen, but I doubt that now – probably closer to eleven or twelve – humiliated nevertheless. It's little wonder that only a few Mexican children were found in the upper grades. Regrettably, most just quit school as soon as the law allowed.

*** *** ***

A most embarrassing event of my young life happened early in the first grade. As I said before, Miz Stapp made the necessary hand signals very clear, and I seldom used the privilege. But this time was different. At first I

32

simply raised my hand – one finger extended. Miz Stapp, either engaged with the second grade or otherwise occupied, failed to look in my direction for quite a while. Time was beginning to be of the essence.

She finally noticed my signal, but politely shook her head and tapped her watch... almost time for recess. She turned back to her task at hand. The old desk seat was soon squeaking from my squirming, and by the time she acknowledged me again, I was waving frantically. "All right, Gus Henry, you may go," she relented. My mind was racing. *Hurry!.. out of the room!* in a panic, *Down the hall – forget the rules, run! – out the side door!* The outhouse stood a 'mile away'! *Why did they have to put the boys' twice as far as the girls'?* I was running as fast as I could when......uh, oh.... It was warm.....and wet.....I had pee-ed in my pants.

At that moment, the bell rang – kids began streaming out the door – RECESS! .... and I..... was.....wet. I slunk behind a tree, waiting for everyone to be preoccupied with their 15 minutes of freedom. Nonchalantly, I sauntered back to the room and stood at the door - Miz Stapp turned from her blackboard. She couldn't help but notice the darkened, damp front of my pants and the tears welling up in my eyes. "Come here, Gus Henry," she beckoned softly. "I'm sorry...now you run home and change...OK?" I nodded, desperately trying to hold back the tears.

Fortunately, home was just down the road. If I ran I might make it back before recess was over. I quickly changed into another pair of jeans while Momma prepared a sandwich and put it in a paper sack along with an apple. "If anyone asks, tell them you came home because you forgot your lunch," she strategized. That noon, while we ate at our desks, no one questioned the shiny black lunch kit, unclaimed and alone on the shelf at the back of the room.

*** *** ***

Not until the threat of cold weather did many of the younger boys (ages 10 or below) wear shoes to school. There wasn't much point. Other than to church, you didn't wear shoes anywhere else in the summertime, and summer often lingered into November. Parents were hardly concerned about the safety of bare feet. Except for a rusty nail in a buried piece of lumber, little could harm the leather-tough sole of a shoe-less waif. Besides, there's the economy of not having to fret about footwear for six months of the year. But come a cold snap, and out came the high-top leather shoes and the ugly black canvas "Keds." Grudgingly we pried them on, hoping for a swift return of the warm, welcome barefoot days of spring.

Large wood-burning stoves heated the classrooms in winter – students sweltered in one corner, shivered in the next. The trustees made certain that an ample supply of firewood was stacked outside. They didn't bother to pile it neatly - just pitched it all into piles creating several tempting mounds of timber, each 'pyramid' silently shouting a compulsive challenge: *"OK guys, who's king of the hill?"*

34

In spite of bruises and scrapes, the recess battles continued until usually two buddies jointly proclaimed their primacy to a summit and the sole right to bore to the base. Then, piece-by-piece, the victors cored the mound, carving out their own little sanctuary of split-oak. The 'spoils' of the core went to the vanquished to fabricate make-shift forts and barricades. Of course, it only lasted until the first blue-norther, when both 'kings' and 'serfs' were obliged to relinquish their claims to the wood stoves in the classrooms.

Two years flew by.

During one summer, however, everything changed. Normally, the school grounds were deserted from June through August. But that year it was alive with activity. Large metal tanks were cemented in place – even larger ones buried with trenches extending into the acreage. People were everywhere – hammering, sawing, digging. In one corner of the property a solitary workman labored hour after hour in the July heat, his well-drilling rig inching deeper and deeper with each thump of the spud. (More about that later.) No one delivered firewood as before.

When we returned that September the building had been transformed. There were restrooms with flushing toilets, drinking fountains in the hallway, butane heaters in the classrooms, a kitchen and dining room with long, heavy, wooden tables and benches. Our little school had been modernized...... But the outhouses remained – just in case.

For an hour before the first PTA meeting that fall the new facilities were open for inspection by the public, including both restrooms. The meeting was abuzz with comments on the improvements. One mother, who had obviously never seen an open horizontal urinal (for simultaneous multi-person use) demanded an explanation: "Why did the boys get bathtubs and not the girls?" Her husband leaned sideways and whispered in her ear. She hid her face for the rest of the meeting.

*** *** ***

We had advanced to the next room down the hall. Grades 3 and 4 - and a new teacher, Miz Jennings – a classic schoolmarm –aging, plump and dowdy. She boarded in the McCann home, neighboring my cousin, Katherine Anne, who made it no secret that she and the new teacher were going to be "very good friends." I knew then that me and Miz J just may not end up on the kindest of terms.

However, the only serious altercation between us came in the form of my disputation of 'facts' presented in our science text regarding the age of the earth and the existence of dinosaurs. I flatly refused to study such rubbish and totally frustrated Miz J's efforts to present the material. I was convinced that she was an atheist and neither she nor the textbook had any place in a good Christian school. Obviously, my folks were quite upset....with me. *I didn't know why! I was taking a stand for the Bible.*

Daddy and Momma weren't going to spend a lot of time debating the issue. "Gus Henry, you don't have to believe everything that's being presented," they said. "But it's well that you learn what others believe, even if you don't. And besides, Miss Jennings is your teacher, and you owe her your respect....now that's the end of it! .... Understand!"

"I guess so," I mumbled, *but I still thought she was an atheist.*

*** *** ***

The fragrance of fresh home-cooking filled the air. The hot meals cost 25 cents a day (two cents extra for milk) or one dollar in advance for a 5-day week. Most mothers welcomed the relief of not having to pack lunches each morning. Other families, especially those with several kids in school, found a dollar a week per child beyond their family's budget. For them, practically every day it was a single peanut butter sandwich – no jelly – and a small apple in a brown paper bag.

The food was simple - nothing fancy - no menu options – but nutritious and sufficient none the less. There were soups, stews – meat casseroles (more casserole than meat) - macaroni cheese with SPAM - hot dogs and burgers alternated on Fridays. But the *piece de resistance* was (drum roll please): BROWN BEANS AND CORNBREAD! Mush them together – add some raw onions and mmm ... mmm! You hope the cook made enough for "seconds."

One never knew the fare for the day until the aromas of the kitchen wafted down the hall. If you didn't like SPAM you took your chances or carried a lunch. However, once a year, near the final week of school they announced, "Friday will be Ice-Cream Day!" Our principal, Mr. Montgomery,

37

arranged for an ice-cream truck to arrive at lunch time. We could have "all the ice-cream you want" – Eskimo pies – popsicles – fudgesicles - dreamsicles - strawberry, chocolate, or vanilla Dixie-cups. Unbelievable? No federal nutritional mandates here. Extravagant? Not really. With an average child devouring five or six items, and the school buying wholesale at less than a nickel apiece, 25 cents would go a long way. Every child was included – even those without a quarter to spare. Today some might call it irresponsible, illegal, and even bordering on child abuse. However Mr. M realized that, although most country kids ate only home-made ice-cream, everyone relished the variety offered that day. What a guy!

*** *** ***

Fourth grade was un-eventful. Miz J was still my teacher, and perhaps not an atheist. Over the summer she had become somewhat pleasant - Katherine Anne wasn't really the "teacher's pet," in spite of the fact that she still thought she was. Milton (the Stark boy with one name) was the only other boy in my grade. Marshall Craig, Pee Wee, and a new kid, JC, were among the third-graders in the room. By now, at recesses we abandoned the east side playground and joined the older boys on the softball field. They despised our limited athletic ability, but without us, they hardly had enough to play, and needed someone to chase 'fly-balls' in the outfield or 'shag' the fouls tipped behind the backstop.

The Stark brothers were talented ball players. Even eight-year-old Pee Wee could outplay most sixth-graders. With nine boys and two spirited sisters in their family, they had enough for a "scrub" game at home themselves. They were all *naturals* on the field.

You could hardly call our school's brigade of athletes a "ball team." Practices consisted of two fifteen-minute recesses each day and whatever time was left on the lunch hour. What amounted to competitive play was a pair of home/away skirmishes each spring against our arch-rivals, the kids from Zion Lutheran in Walburg.

Using every boy in grades five thru eight, Mr. Montgomery still couldn't put together a total of nine to round-out a squad. So he'd recruit Milton and Pee Wee from Miz J's room. And that meant that Marshall Craig, JC, and I were left behind. I must admit, I was a little more than jealous. But, I vowed that things would be different the following year. I'd be one year older, one grade higher and, except for Pee Wee, the boys in Miz J's room would be little threat to my improved ball-playing skills. I'd show them! I couldn't help but amaze them, since I have my authentic cow-hide, autographed Ted Williams glove.

*** *** ***

Fifth Grade! Miz Margaret was unlike any schoolmarm I'd ever seen..... I couldn't call her Miz. She's nothing like Miz Stapp or Miz J. She's a genuine "Miss". Progressing to her classroom was a dream come true – not just for me but for other guys too. She was young and beautiful, with coal–black hair and a shapely figure that belied her occupation. I could hardly believe I'd finally made it to fifth grade with Miss Margaret....*I think I'll stop going barefoot.*

A strange thing, you know, it must have been the weather that summer of 1949. The girls in our class returned a lot cuter and prettier than they were three months earlier.

The ball team? Oh, yes, the ball team – no problem. Several of best players had graduated from the eighth grade the previous spring. A spot on the team was a cinch – glove or no glove.

Other interests came to the forefront as well. The county book-mobile library rolled in every two weeks and juvenile books no longer caught our attention. For real mature reading we passed around the limited number of *Hardy Boy Mysteries*, the latest copies of *Popular Mechanics,* and the biographies of inventors and scientists. At some point every boy in the room painted Tom Sawyer's fence and rafted down the Mississippi with Huck and Jim.

We all joined the 4-H Club, a national organization that focused on leadership, responsible citizenship, and the development of practical skills. We met once a month after school to hear lectures and advice from 'experts' and give our reports on the projects we had adopted. The girls concentrated mostly on domestic skills while the boys' emphases were raising some type of livestock. We were to purchase our 'project' – feed it - care for it - keep records of expenditures, production and the like - and at the end of the year determine the profit our 'project' had realized.

Marshall Craig chose pigs.
My folks suggested…chickens.

The plan they proposed was to give me an interest-free 'loan' to 'buy' the family's current flock. At the end of the year they would 'buy' it back, so I could pay the 'loan.' Simple enough…but then everything else was my responsibility. Rain or shine, every day demanded gathering the eggs, feeding and 'watering.' I bought the feed on credit from Jacobs Store, and 'sold' most of the eggs to Daddy to pay for the feed. The rest went to Momma's kitchen. There were the required records to keep: initial investment, cost of materials and feed, eggs gathered, chicks hatched, etc. And, of course, every month the 'droppings' had to be scraped from the roosts and floor of the hen-house and hauled away.

When I finally closed the books on the venture, my parents bought back my flock, and I 'paid off' the loan. The eggs sold to the store did manage to cover the feed bill ….barely. Most of the profit was eaten up….literally. The bottom line of my record book showed a total gain of $8.73 – I had shoveled all of those droppings and realized less than a dollar per month.

Marshall Craig took $50.00 to the bank.

*** *** ***

I arrived at school early that first day of the sixth year. Miss Margaret was nowhere around. I took a seat in the back. She entered a few moments later, smelling of roses or lilacs or something. She was more radiant than ever. "Good morning! Gus Henry," she cheerfully quipped, mussing my hair as she passed. *She likes me!. .She really likes me!*

41

This is going to be the BEST school year of my life!

The bell rang - the others came in and took their places. "Before we begin," she smiled, "I have a surprise for you! While you were having fun all summer, so was I." She raised her left hand – a shiny little flash from one finger. "I GOT MARRIED!" she exclaimed. The girls all screamed with excitement and rushed to her desk ……. I just sat there….. slack-jawed and speechless.

This is going to be the WORST school-year of my life!

Recovery from the 'jilting' took a couple of weeks. Then life went on much the same as before. Miss Margaret remained a very pretty lady with coal-black hair and a shapely figure that belied her profession. And she liked me…she really liked me. But she was a married woman now…so… oh, well…

44

TELLING OFF THE PREZ

M y older sister insisted that I include an incident of which I have no personal recollection. But Vangie swears it happened. She calls it: *"The time Gus Henry told-off the President of the United States."*

*** *** ***

Every parent's stern admonition, "BEHAVE YOUR-SELF," negated the necessity for my first-grade teacher, Miz Stapp to have a written list of 'do's and don'ts'. If she needed a new rule, she'd make it up on the spot. Early on, she did stress three most important items:
NO RUNNING IN THE HALL -
NO BUBBLE GUM UNDER THE SEAT OF YOUR DESK
(*but where can you put it when it still has juice left in it?*)
NO JUMPING OFF THE AUDITORIUM STAGE.

In the mid-1940's Lyndon B. Johnson was the U.S. Representative in Washington for our neck of the woods. LBJ never shirked an opportunity to win voters – current or future – even at a dusty crossroads-to-nowhere called Andice. I don't know if it was an evening rally or one of those school 'assemblies.' Either way, you can be sure that the room was packed with folks from all over – standing room only. Six year old 'little me' was seated on the floor somewhere down front.

Introductions completed, the confident congressman strode forward, and, with little effort, leapt on stage – a low vault of 18-20 inches from the auditorium floor.

Following his oration the 'famous' politician was anxious to 'press the flesh' (his term for a political hand-shake) and he literally hopped off the stage. No sooner had he jumped down, than Vangie's little brother jumped up and shook his finger in stern admonishment of the guest of honor, "Hey, mister!" he warned, " Don't you let Miz Stapp catch you jumping off that stage. She'll whup you for sure!" The crowd roared with laughter, and, I'd like to think, so did the future president.

48

WATER WITCHING

One day in May, the school year almost done, we went out at recess to find a man walking back and forth on the playground. He held a forked willow branch tightly with both hands - waist high in front of him - horizontal to the ground - his grip, palms-upward.

After lunch he was still there but spending his time in a smaller area of the grounds. He'd walk slowly - the point of the willow would begin to wiggle. He'd stop...then walk a little further - walk... wiggle ... walk... wiggle ... all of sudden!! The point end of the branch turned straight down and it appeared that, with his awkward grip, he didn't have the strength to turn it up again. He placed it on the ground at the spot where it had indicated and stacked a pile of rocks on top. With a steely glare he turned, pointed at the stones, then aimed his gaunt finger at us and growled, "There's water down there. Don't any of you dare to move those rocks!"

"N-n-no, sir!" we promised. *Just wait 'till I get home and tell the folks what happened.*

The first week in June, the school year over, the man came with a well digging rig and began to work right over his sacred spot. No powered augers - the process was slow, hot and loud. With long summer days and nothing to do, Craig and I would at times go and watch the man - "Not too close," he warned with a grimace, then smile, nod and return to his task. By the end of July the hole was some six-hundred feet deep. Pipes, an electric pump and a water tank had taken the place of the rocks, the willow branch and the man with his noisy rig. Andice School now had fresh water for a kitchen and rest rooms and bubbly drinking fountains and mop buckets and flower pots in windows and...

Don't tell me it didn't happen. It's called "water witching." It amazed me as a boy and, as an adult, I've seen it repeated. Other than what I've just said, I won't attempt to explain it.

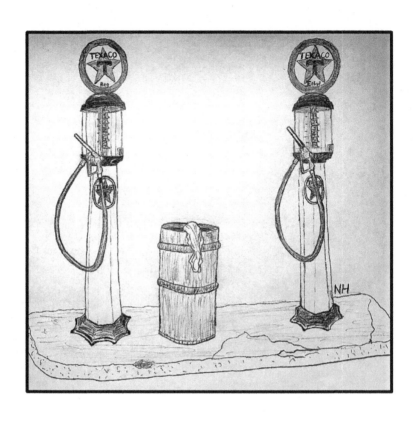

DOC'S GAS PUMP

I t was years before 'Doc' Davis installed an electric gas pump at his garage. Originally he had two hand-operated pumps in front of his small shop – one for REGULAR - one for ETHYL. They were called Visible Pumps, not for their obvious presence, like sentries standing on concrete pads, but 'visible' because the customers could see what they were getting – gasoline flowing from a 10- gallon glass cylinder near the top of the unit. Inside the cylinder a bronze rod with metal tabs set at gallon intervals, measured the flow.

Each pump, topped with a milk-glass globe, proudly proclaimed the brand that 'Doc' was selling at the time. As his suppliers changed, only the globe was replaced. Over time 'Doc' sold SINCLAIR, with its green dinosaur mascot, GULF – HUMBLE – TEXACO – the familiar brands in the area. Newer citified pumps were electric, with globes that lit up at night. 'Doc' just figured, "What good would that do me? By dark I'll have locked up and be home for supper!"

A hand-rocked lever pumped gasoline from a large underground tank. Dispensing began with the glass cylinder filled to ten gallons. Few customers needed more. If they did you filled the glass another time. The hose and nozzle were nothing automatic. Just thrust the tube into the customer's tank, flip the trigger and watch as the gas level dropped in the cylinder, one bronze tab per gallon. (And, if you drained the glass, be sure to drain the hose as well.)

Self-service was common – a holler would come through the door, "Hey 'Doc' I got a gallon and a pack of Juicy Fruit – put it on my tab!" Sweating under the hood of a jalopy, without even lifting his gaze, 'Doc' would nod, wave and continue tinkering. Highly unlikely that someone else would come along for a while. He would add 30 cents to the customer's credit book later – a quarter for the gas – a nickel for the gum.

So, what made 'Doc's' pumps special? Watching the cylinder fill – the pump lever - PUUULL ("shuuch" - sucking gas from below) – PUUUSH -red/orange liquid swooched and foamed as it inched up the glass. PUUULL - PUUSH PUULL - PUUSH. Amazing!

And… there was the time he called to an eight year old kid, imitating the pump-lever motion from his dad's storefront across the road…

"Wanna give it a try?

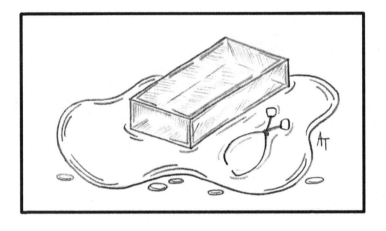

THE ICE MAN

"Hey! It's the iceman!"

That's Craig, my best friend, the only boy in town near my age. He's nine – I'm ten and we're high-tailing it for Dollahan's store. With a little bit of luck, and if we stay out of the way, and if the ice man is not running late and if he's feeling generous, we just might end up with a couple of chunks of ice the size of our fists to cool us on a hot summer day.

Water from melting ice dripped from his truck to the ground below. It wasn't refrigerated like modern ones today - just an ordinary old truck with wooden sides and an open bed covered with a layer of straw. Under a heavy tarp lay the ice, each mass weighing at least 300 pounds. Uncovered, they glistened in the sunlight like huge blocks of glass – rainbows reflecting from deep within.

The driver maneuvered his vehicle to an outside dock and dropped a ramp from the truck to the door of the icehouse. With large tongs he dragged a heavy block to the rear of the truck, running the leading edge of the ice over the lip of the ramp. Pinching the sharp tongs into the back of the block, he heaved it upward and let it slide into the building. Stay back! A solid block of ice at full speed down a ramp can be deadly.

The ice house – a small windowless, wooden building - walls, floor and ceiling eight to ten inches thick, was insulated with straw (fiberglass and styrofoam were unknown). Its heavy door, as thick as the walls, closed the building to the summer heat. Inside all was cool – the closest thing to air-conditioning for miles around.

As I recall, each block of ice measured a foot thick, two feet wide, and four feet long, with several indented ridges down the sides. No one ever bought a full 300 pound block of ice, and the ridges allowed it to be chopped into smaller blocks. Since large blocks don't melt as quickly as smaller ones, the ice was kept in full blocks until sold. Several hard ice-pick jabs along the side and the block broke neatly into smaller sections. For an additional charge, Mr. Dollahan would crush the purchase with his rusty old hand-cranked "crusher." Most however, bought their ice in 25 pound blocks and chipped it themselves, if needed.

In rural areas, like Andice, ice was essential in those days. Many families, on their weekly trip to town, would buy a small block, wrap it in a burlap bag and tote it home as quickly as possible. Little, if any, went into drinks for the family. Iced tea and cold lemonade were rare treats. Even rarer yet was a fresh churn of homemade ice cream.

Electricity was available to most homes at that time, but some continued to keep perishables in their "ice box," a large vertical wooden cabinet that held ice and the few items that had to be kept cool and fresh for more than a day. To be certain the ice lasted as long as possible, mother was the only one allowed to open the box, and only when necessary.

The ice man and his truck always arrived on Friday, since most families would come to town for necessities on Saturday. In time, Mr. Dollahan didn't sell all of his weekly stock. Inside the thick walls, blocks slowly shrank and profit melted away. More people were buying electric refrigerators, although they continued to call them "ice boxes."

Then, one Friday, the ice man didn't come – and he didn't come the next week – or any week thereafter. Craig and I no longer rushed to Dollahan's with hopes of frozen refreshment. The thick-walled, wooden structure stood useless. As time passed the heavy door could barely swing on its corroded hinges. The rusty old ice crusher had disappeared long ago. Eventually someone bought the building to use as fireplace fuel in a new brick home. Ironic: wood and timbers that once held back the summer heat, now died as flames of warmth against the winter cold.

SUMMER AT GRANDMA KELM'S

Just beyond Walburg - a few miles east of Possum Creek stood the two-story country, farm home of my maternal grandmother Kelm. Summer Sundays were the most memorable times there. Cousin Lawrence lived in a small house adjacent, and thus, whenever I was at Grandma's, so was he.

Grandma lived alone in her big house. Grandpa had died years before I was born, and their children (Momma and her siblings) were all married with families of their own. The bedrooms on the second floor were left closed, unused and intriguing. Most of the furniture remained – beds, chairs, cluttered dusty wardrobes, and bureau drawers filled with odds and ends - treasures from years gone by.

Downstairs in the parlor, stood an old player piano. I don't know what we enjoyed more: pumping the wheezing bellows for the punch-paper rolls or spinning up and down on the screw-posted piano stool. Grandma busied herself in the kitchen. And summers meant fresh plum jellies, apricot jam, pear-butter, and Grandma's delicious peach pie[2] – fruit from the orchard on the other side of the barn, where Uncle Bert tended the animals.

A shallow hand-dug well, 20-30 feet deep, had been the only source for water when Momma was a child. The

---

[2] See Appendix for Grandma's peach pie recipe

advent of electricity brought a deep well and modern plumbing. But the old one still served a purpose. Grandma kept her butter in the wooden bucket, lowered to just above the water line some 20 feet below. Even in the heat of summer, the temperature of the well at that depth remained a cool 75 degrees – cool enough to keep butter fresh for days and soft enough to spread easily on hot fresh biscuits.

A small stream meandered its way through the pasture. On its slippery banks scores of hollow mud turrets, several inches high, marked the entrances to crawfish burrows. The stream was too shallow for perch, so the alternative was to fish for the "mud bugs." Lawrence would look for lengths of string while I begged a slice or two of bacon from Grandma. There was nothing complicated about crawfishing: tie a bit of bacon on the end of the string, drop it down the hollow turret, wait for a gentle tug and pull up the catch.

As with any fishing expedition, the results always varied – sometimes a few, sometimes a lot. But one or two were always enough to terrify the girls and disgust the women. Those miniature lobsters had a menacing look when held between two fingers – their claws waving and threatening.

From time to time we would make our way to Possum Creek where the water ran cool over its rocky bed. In places it was deep and wide enough for swimming. Most of the time, however, our objective was the limestone outcroppings along its banks. Searching for gold, certain that, although we failed many times before, we were, like prospectors of old, unrelenting in our quest. After all, years ago it was reported that a nugget had been found.

Finally, we "struck it rich." After hours of chipping away at limestone and scouring through the shallows, there it was, bright and gleaming in the sun! Just a palm-sized stone embedded with shiny specks – small, but worth all our efforts. In a few minutes we were back at the farm. In a few seconds our rapture was deflated – iron pyrite – "fool's gold."

One mid-afternoon a terrible shriek was heard coming from outside. Momma and the aunts streamed out of the back door. Daddy and the uncles came running from their croquet match. Cousin Lawrence stood at the barnyard gate, blood streaming down his face. "What happened!" everyone shouted in chorus. "Horace! ...Horace...!" he managed to mutter. "Horace kicked me...right here." pointing to his forehead, where a small gash proved the source of the gore. Daddy and Uncle Bert rushed him to town. Doc Wiedermeier sewed a few stiches, prescribed some aspirin and sent him home "fit as a fiddle."

What happened to Horace? Oh, I forgot to mention that Horace was the family's mule.

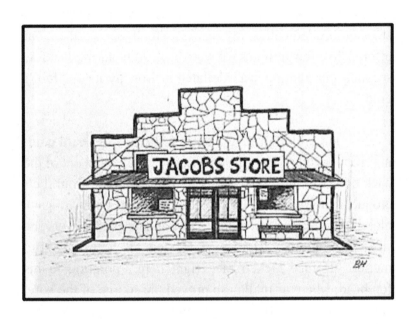

JACOBS STORE

They don't make them like that anymore! I'm referring to the enterprise my dad and Uncle Ben operated in Andice for some 42 years. The structure is gone, having burned to the ground several years after the brothers retired. Only a few photographs and a vacant spot remain. I walk its original perimeter and step through where the front door had been and now it all seems so small.

The building itself was a wooden structure with a tin roof. The double front door and two large store-front windows penetrated its pink granite façade. A covered porch ran the width of the building where a wooden bench provided outdoor seating in the heat of summer and lazy rainy days. Carved in the bench were numerous names and initials, hearts and arrows - occasionally a vulgarism appeared and was expeditiously obliterated.

The porch was more than a place for husbands to linger on Saturdays as their wives shopped for weekly vittles. It was a convenient local "stump" for politicians from county judges to U.S. senators. Long before he became president, Lyndon Johnson frequented Andice and held forth in his bid for election on the front porch of Jacobs Store. (He never knew that Daddy was a Republican).

Daddy had begun the venture and the original sign proclaimed GUS F JACOB GENERAL MERCHANDISE.

It remained that way for many years, even after Uncle Ben became a full partner with every dollar divided 50/50 between the two brothers. Eventually, when the lettering grew faint and a new marquee was required, a simple JACOBS STORE became its identity.

In many ways it was like the Godsey's store in the *The Waltons* television series. Food stuffs lined one wall – an ice cream box and candy counter were among the first things you encountered - the "soda waters" were all the way to the back - bananas hung on a single three-foot stalk – in the center section were counters of dry goods. Shelves on the opposite wall held shoes for men and boys – work shoes and mud boots for the most part, but also black KEDS high-top sneakers.

The ladies could buy yards of cloth, pins, buttons, zippers, needles, thread, brik-a-brack, etc., etc. If someone needed a 10 foot-long 'cotton-pickin' sack, Daddy would just cut a 20 foot length of heavy canvas cloth. One section of the wall was devoted to drug items – from Castor Oil to Hadacol – some concoctions, legitimate at the time, would be cause for prosecution today.

In a corner, farther back, were shelves of paint and other supplies – most every small tool a farming family might need – ax handles and axes, hammers and pliers, hoes, shovels and spades - buckets and tubs – mops and brooms, rakes and rat traps. A new Maytag washing machine stood proudly on the floor, posing for a buyer.

A small spot next to a window was Daddy's "office." *The Wall Street Journal*, the *Fort Worth Star Telegram,* and a myriad of other papers piled on his desk. His heavy safe, often laden with cotton samples, was within arm's reach of his wobbly swivel chair. As a cotton broker Daddy bought bales of cotton from the local gin, sent the samples for agents to examine, then shipped the bales to Galveston. Even in this enterprise he shared the profits with his brother.

The rear storage area held goods waiting to be shelved plus additional hardware – kegs of nails, a large multi-drawered carrousel with every size of nut, bolt, and washer – pipe and pipe fittings. Although Doc Davis sold gas for cars and trucks, kerosene was a "grocery" item, and Jacobs' Store had an adequate supply in a fifty-gallon tank. Its utility diminished as the years passed, and only on occasion would a little old lady bring in her gallon "coal-oil" can for a refill.

Hundred pound sacks of milled livestock feed and fifty pound sacks of flour for baking were stacked against a wall. Every sack was made from quality cotton cloth, printed in various colors - some with floral patterns, others striped or checkered. Every bag of "mash" contained the identical mixture of feed. However, the missus of the house jealously held to her privilege and responsibility to personally decide which bag to buy. Home-sewn shirts and skirts - once feed and flour sacks - were common attire in the school classroom in those days. More often than not, the floral pattern she had in mind was at the bottom of the pile, and you had to move a ton of chicken mash to retrieve her selection – only to have her change her mind for the one that had been at the top of the stack, which was now– *you guessed it* - at the bottom.

On the other hand, it was very likely that she didn't see the design she required. The sack bought two weeks before had just not quite enough material to complete her project and we didn't have another sack like it. *"Oh, my! Now I'll have to run to Florence to see if Daniell's Store has it."* She'd leave in a huff with her entire grocery order on the check-out counter. Such were the trials of a country merchant.

The "nerve center" – where Daddy spent the majority of his time was the meat market. Each day began with sharpening knives – some blades used so often that what once might have been as broad as a chef's knife were eventually honed to stiletto thinness. Meats were displayed in a single refrigerated case – steaks, hamburger, pork chops, roasts, liver, heart, tongue, brains and kidneys – all from animals raised and slaughtered by Uncle Ben. A large round butcher-block was the working table. Before acquiring an electric band saw, every steak had to be cut by hand. Bones, with slender traces of meat attached, ended up in a cardboard box under the block. My dog Smack, and the other canines in town, ate very well.

My father took great pride in his work, but probably none greater than in his "home-made" sausage, blended with his own recipe of spices and smoked as only he knew how (a treasured German tradition). In addition to local patrons, customers from as distant as Houston and Dallas, called in

68

advance to reserve what they could, and in season, hunters from far and wide brought deer to be processed into his celebrated venison sausage.

During the coldest days of winter, local folks and farmers with time on their hands, would sit around the single wood-burning stove, share gossip and watch Daddy convert a hindquarter of beef into steaks and roasts. In the meantime, they might order a sandwich – ham or cheese for 10 cents a slice – 15 cents for two, Daddy would cut the bologna, toast the bread, and spread some mustard or mayo. Another 10 cents would get them a Coke and a bag of chips. For only a quarter: a sandwich, chips, and Coke. Quite a deal!

*** *** ***

For as long as the store existed, it had no toilet. The only facility available was the "two-hole" outhouse on the back of the property. It was frequented by many, since it was the only public outhouse in town. I never really understood the necessity of its being a "two-holer." I don't ever recall anyone, myself especially, simultaneously sharing the convenience. I always considered its greatest danger lay in the fact that the area beneath the "comfort holes" was not tightly enclosed and that one's bare posterior was exposed to any number of perils, especially wasps, scorpions, spiders, and snakes. It had been overturned a number of times – not by wind or other storm – its upending, for a number of years, had become the annual ritual of various Halloween pranksters.

*** *** ***

The store was my father's life – six days a week, Monday thru Saturday – open at 6:30 or 7:00 in the morning – close no earlier than twelve hours later and as late as 10:00 or after on Saturday. He'd walk the two hundred yards home for lunch and in summertime, take a 20 minute nap, then, back to work. Rarely did he take a vacation.

In a retirement interview Daddy recalled business in the 1930's:

> "When we first opened," he said, "150 pounds of sugar sold for $3.85 - eggs were 7 cents a dozen and 50 pounds of flour, 79 cents...two pounds of hamburger went for 25 cents...A man could buy a pair of overalls for 89 cents, but he had to work a full day to earn that much." [3]

Credit had always been the mainstay of independent merchants and shopkeepers. Today, the risk is assumed by credit card companies and banks. In Daddy's day, the owner alone was vulnerable, dependent solely on the "good faith" of the customer. In 1974 Daddy and Uncle Ben sold the store and retired, forfeiting uncollected credit charges that, in a 21st century economy, would be well within a six figure total.

Late on Saturdays, Daddy would lock up. With the week's receipts tucked under his arm he'd walk home in the dark, never fearing harm or loss. Spreading it all on the kitchen table, he would total the cash as we kids rolled the

---

[3] L. Ashbrook, *The Austin American-Statesman,* July 28, 1974

coins for deposit. But before all was put aside, Daddy would select several of the crispest bills and seal them in a small envelope for church the next morning.

Many a Sunday there was a knock on the door of our home – someone "desperately in need of a loaf of bread." Daddy never refused. By the time he unlocked the store the petitioner would have "forgotten" the bread but remembered a more urgent scarcity: a pack of cigarettes. Leaving quickly he'd call back, "Charge it, Gus!" Daddy would add the charge to an already lengthy list in the customer's credit booklet, knowing full well it would be months – if ever – before the purchase was cleared.

Even if there were no "Sunday customers," we'd often make a quick stop at the store before heading to church. Daddy had to have several packages of gum ready for handouts to children at church after the service. Standing aside, the kids would impatiently wait for Daddy to conclude his small talk with the other men. Then he'd turn and step toward the youngsters - a rush to his side, hands outstretched and eyes wide open. He loved it!

GETTING OUR NICKLE'S WORTH

How lucky can one get! To be a "kid in a candy store" – anything you want. That's what some cousins thought of me, because my father owned a grocery. Not only did he have a soda water box and an ice cream case, there was that counter filled with every candy bar and sugar treat imaginable. True, that stuff was within our reach but it was not within our grasp.

In the first place, you must remember that although the sign on the establishment read *Gus F. Jacob – General Merchandise,* Daddy was only half owner – the other half was his brother's. To make sure there was equity in the families, Daddy and Uncle Ben had agreed that their children of school age could each select five cents worth of any sweet each day after school.

In those days, with a nickel you could purchase almost anything from the counter – *Baby Ruth – Milky Way – Snickers – Butterfinger –* all for a nickel. Every soft drink in the ice chest, 5 cents. A single scoop of ice cream – your choice of flavors as long as it was vanilla, chocolate or strawberry – or maybe a "Dixie Cup" of ice cream with a picture of a movie star on the inside of the lid. Just peel off a paper liner and you had a round trading card. Save 10 lids and return them to the address given, along with a 3-cent stamp and in several weeks an autographed 8x10 photo of the star of your choice arrived in the mail.

It took a long time to accumulate 10 lids, even if I had to rummage through the store's waste bin or wash the dirt from those lying outside in the dust. But in time Roy Rodgers, Gene Autry, and Hopalong Cassidy were smiling down from the ceiling above my bed.

As I was saying, each day we were allowed only a "nickel's worth." And Uncle Ben's watchful eye made sure it was <u>only</u> a "nickel's worth." If one skipped the previous day, a ten-cent item was permitted – two scoops of ice cream, or a 5 cent bag of peanuts poured into a bottle of *Coke* – a treat that at age eighty I still enjoy.

There was another very unusual item for dime – a small round box of Spanish peanuts – about two inches tall and one inch wide. There weren't any more nuts in these boxes than in a regular 5-cent bag (maybe even less). But, with your purchase you had the chance to find, with the nuts, a penny, nickel, dime, or in some rare cases a dollar bill, tightly folded inside. Customers would shake each little box to find the one that sounded different, hoping that it held something other than the "goobers." You knew the result when you heard them cry, "NUTS!" Occasionally the re-ward was a penny. I was told that someone once actually found a one-dollar bill. True or not, the thought of possibly "striking it rich" in a box of peanuts was something to dream about, especially for a youngster who was only allowed a "nickel's worth."

SODA WATER

Everyone called anything in the drink cooler a "coke." The" Yankees" from "up north" called it "pop". But I'll always remember the big red cooler in the back corner of Daddy's store as the box that held the 'soda water'.

Long before any of us ever heard of vending machines, the soda water box was the first place customers headed to on a hot day. It was simply a thick wooden box with a watertight metal-lined interior. A hinged lid kept out the warm air and a valve in the bottom drained the melted ice, since the drinks were chilled by a daily supply of fresh ice chipped by hand from a fifty-pound block. The outside was bright red with the familiar Coca-Cola script on the sides. Thousands of boxes, just like the one Daddy had, were furnished to stores everywhere by the Coca-Cola Company.

After school – and early on summer mornings – it was my responsibility to make sure the water was drained and the box was filled - similar drinks together, upright with bottle necks and caps visible above the ice. About one-fourth of the cooler was for Cokes with the rest of the space for Dr. Pepper, Royal Crown (RC) Cola, Pepsi, 7-Up, Orange Crush, Grapette, Hires Root Beer, and Nehi strawberry. Not a single diet drink in the bunch, and nothing in cans or plastic. Any drink of your choosing was only 5 cents – from the 6 ounce bottle of Coke to the big 12 ounce Pepsi – only a nickel – plus an extra two-cent 'bottle deposit' if you wanted to take the drink with you.

Back then there were only two ways you could get a Coke: (1) the fancy way – spritzed from a nozzle at a drug store soda fountain or (2) in the familiar shapely bottle. The Coca-Cola Company made only one product – COKE. Nothing more – no Fanta, no Sprite, no Pibb, no caffeine-free – just one flavor – Coke. Dr. Pepper and the others, RC and 7-Up, produced the grape, orange, strawberry, and root beer.

All bottlers delivered their drinks in wooden cases - 24 bottles per. As empty bottles accumulated, the cases of empties were stacked outside in back of the store – bottles from different companies mixed together in various cases. My job - sort the empties into their appropriate cases for the delivery drivers to pick up on their next round - Coke bottles in Coke cases - Dr. Pepper bottles to Dr. Pepper cases, etc. You see, the bottles were used over and over again – empties returned to the bottler for washing and refilling.

No one questioned the efficiency of the cleaning process. Empty bottles went back in numerous unsanitary states - lipstick on the rims and all sorts of who-knows-what inside – bubble gum, unfinished drinks, cigarette butts, mud, worms, insects, chewing tobacco, and things not polite to mention. We were a trusting generation. No one knew - or cared - whose lips had last touched the mouth of a bottle or what slime it had previously contained.

The sorting job wasn't a complete bore, however – thanks to Coca-Cola with its bottling plants all over the nation, and the world. Whenever Coke placed an order for a shipment of new bottles, the name of the city, in which they were first to be filled, was molded in glass on the bottom of the bottle. Most of the Coke bottles we saw had AUSTIN TEX on the bottom, and it was not uncommon to see a DALLAS or SAN ANTONIO. Once in a while, however, I would come across CHICAGO or NEW ORLEANS or MIAMI or a city I had never even heard of.

Coke bottles travelled all over the country as people paid their 2 cents for Cokes "to go"- keeping the empty as deposit for another Coke farther down the road. I once imagined an empty bottle, stamped PHILADELPHIA, PA found stuck in the mud in back of Jacobs Store in Andice, Texas, refilled in Austin, sold in Lukenbach and elsewhere again and again, eventually finding its final resting place, chipped and broken in a dirty dumpster behind Rose's Cantina in El Paso - never to return to its home in the "City of Brotherly Love."

THE CIRCUS

Were there ever nights in your childhood when you just couldn't go to sleep – not for fear of the "boogy man" or that something you ate was now eating you or even some pangs of conscience you knew you had to confess before "they" learned the truth? No, what I am referring to is the blessed insomnia of the anticipated thrill of what the morrow would bring – a birthday – or Christmas – or, even better: you knew that the circus had arrived and you were going to be there within a few hours!

The circuses are all gone now – at least the best ones. Ringling Brothers & Barnum and Bailey – *The Greatest Show on Earth* – closed - only a memory (after almost 150 years of performances). To get a sense of what it once was, I recommend the 1952 movie by the same name. The plot is a little "hokey" but the grandeur of its setting is accurate. Television and other forms of entertainment today have led to the demise of this exciting spectacle. It was the Ringling Brothers who kept me awake that night.

Several weeks before, I had gone to Georgetown with Momma for some reason – maybe it was my piano lesson (UGH) when all of a sudden! Outside on a warehouse wall, which last trip had only been clapboard and fading paint, a life-sized tiger was jumping through a hoop directly at me. The full-color poster screamed....

RINGLING BROS. & BARNUM AND BAILEY CIRCUS
THE GREATEST SHOW ON EARTH

AUSTIN, TEXAS – OCTOBER 4 & 5

Two days only....and it's just a month away. That's hardly enough time to break your parents' indifference to one of the fundamental needs of your childhood development. After all, the circus only came every two years and we missed it last time.

I don't know how I finally convinced them, but we were going. That would mean I would have to skip school that day, although teachers didn't get too bent out of shape about those things back then. There was only one hitch – my behavior. I've got to avoid a "whupping" for next three weeks?.....O PLEEEEZE....!

Wide awake at the first light of dawn. The forty mile trip to Austin was an eternity. I *know* Daddy drove slower than usual just to aggravate me. When we arrived, there it was! The gigantic tent – a time when the circus still performed under the "big top" – five large rings of circus acts all going at once – the high wire act – the trapeze – lions – elephants – acrobatic dogs & horses – and clown, clowns, and more clowns. It was unbelievable! No one minded or even noticed the hard wooden bleachers we had for seats. It was one of the most amazing sights I had ever seen.

For the next few weeks, I lived that day over and over again. I tried to get my poor dog, Smack, to substitute as lion, tiger, elephant or whatever, to my commands as the great animal trainer I saw myself to be. He just sat there with a puzzled look on his face. But it didn't matter to me – I knew the world I was in, and it was enough if good old Smack just served as audience.

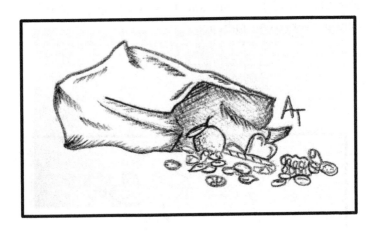

THE CHRISTMAS BAG

T here was an old Christmas custom among many German Lutheran churches, especially those in small towns and rural communities. It may also have been observed by others, but I'm not sure.

Christmas Eve at Zion was always special. A cedar tree had been cut from a nearby woods and its lights and fragrance had filled the church since the first week in Advent. But on Christmas Eve another aroma greeted our nostrils as we entered the door. The Christmas Bags! We couldn't see them but we knew they were there - somewhere - manifest by the fragrance of their contents.

The schoolchildren had prepared a special program for the celebration - telling again the story of the Child in the manger. And there were the old Christmas Carols - in German and English. All of us kids could hardly wait for it to end and be handed that special treat at the end of the service - The Christmas Bag - one for each child as they exited the church - a bag of special goodies.

It was simply an ordinary brown paper bag. But inside - an orange, an apple, some years a tangerine as well, ribbon candy and hard candies of various colors and flavors. Perhaps best of all were the nuts - Brazil nuts, almonds, hazelnuts, walnuts, pecans - three or four of each, all in their shells. And, of course, a candy cane or two.

In the 21st Century that doesn't seem like anything special. But back then...

The custom originated long before I was born. It may have been brought from Europe. It was a time when such treats were rarely experienced by many children, especially in winter. During the years of the Great Depression in the 1930's, the paper bag handed to children at church was likely the only gift some of them opened at Christmas.

The Church Christmas Committee always had the problem of how many bags to prepare. They knew every member's child would be there, but how many visitors could they expect? Too many bags would be extravagant - too few would be embarrassing. More than once my siblings and I came home with only a single bag between us - or none at all. Daddy would come to the car and retrieve our treasure trove, explaining, "You can get all the candy and fruit you need in our store. There weren't enough bags to go around, this time."

As the years passed the volume of goodies became less, and the bags themselves got smaller. Although the "old folks" cherished the tradition, they had to admit that the fruits, sweets and nuts, once so rare, were becoming readily available all year 'round, hardly something special any more. As each Christmas season approached, long and heated debates ensued among committee members and church officers. *How much longer should the custom continue?* Obviously, the Rubicon had to be crossed. Some congregations surrendered early - others held on until a new century was about to dawn. Like corsets and mustache wax the Christmas Bag was ultimately relegated to the dust bin of history.

CHRISTMAS AT GRANDMA JACOB'S

Nothing could compare to Christmas at Grandma's. After church we headed for her house, the one she shared with my Aunt Esther, Uncle Albert and their four boys. Grandma would stay at home to cook; she rarely went to church with the family, since she was totally deaf, having lost her hearing as a young mother.

Everyone hoped that by this time of year at least one "norther" will have blown into Texas, ushering in the hog butchering season. You had to have cold weather – processing pork in the open air on a warm day was impractical. Uncle Albert would take advantage of the chill. The ham, bacon and sausage to be hung and cured. The smell of the smokehouse, its inner walls blackened by years of oak-wood smoke, teased our nostrils as we approached Grandma's back door.

Myriad aromas filled the house: roasted turkey – ginger and sugar cookies – the fragrance of fruit and cedar. The tree had been cut, mounted and decorated with real apples, oranges, candy canes. Long strings of popcorn encircled the tree. Electric "bubble lights" illuminated its branches. Everything said *wilkomen* (welcome)!

For us kids the top priority was the parlor, to scrutinize the packages piled around the tree. In the large, wide hallway the uncles set up card tables for dominoes after dinner, while the women scurried around the kitchen. Uncle Albert would break out his home-made wine to pour servings for everyone – and in true German tradition, even the children were favored with sips.

At least sixteen adults could wedge around the dining room table. Younger children and a mother or two ate in the kitchen. Although she was deaf, Grandma said the blessing in German and plates began to fill. Platters and bowls were passed across and around the table until Aunt Olga was handed the gravy three times, and she still had nothing to put it on. She rose to put a stop to the chaos. "OK! EVERY-BODY!" she declared, taking command, "Everything goes to your left -- clockwise -- LEFT!" Turkey – dressing - ham – potatoes – green beans – fresh bread - yeast rolls - English peas - cranberry sauce - noodles (must always have noodles) – and gravy, lots and lots of gravy.

Except for the cranberries and coffee, everything on the table was homegrown and homemade. Dessert was offered, but practically no one accepted the invitation, so the sweets remained on display: candies, cookies; peach, apple and pumpkin pies; angel food and chocolate cakes; banana and tapioca puddings. Gradually, throughout the afternoon, the selections began to dwindle, as passers-by found room for "just a bite."

Following dinner, the children were "shooed" out-doors. The men had their games of "42" or Cribbage, while the women scrubbed dishes in the kitchen. Later, everyone was beckoned to the parlor. You didn't have to call us twice. It was time to open presents. But wait! A solemn reminder from one of the uncles of the "reason for the season," and Grandma, in spite of her deafness, would sing an old German Christmas song, drawn from deep in the memories of her childhood. Although I didn't understand the language, I was amazed that she maintained a familiar melody fairly well.

Each grandchild received a single gift from the grandparents – always something special. I'll never forget the time my cousin, Ollie, and I were given identical *Hohner Harmonicas* and then immediately dismissed from the gathering. This year, something much quieter - identical leather baseball gloves, with Ted William's autograph in the palm. We spent the rest of the afternoon "breaking them in"- molding a perfect pocket for the ball.

Supper was as big a spread as the one a few hours earlier. This time no one sat around the table, but filled paper plates and ate wherever convenient. Platters were piled high with hot smoked sausage, sour kraut, more fresh bread from the oven, and bowls of *smearkase*, [4] the soft mellow cheese that could have only come from Grandma's kitchen. These, and left-overs from noon, became the evening meal – adding, of course, more sweets, including warm *kafekuchen*,

---

[4] See Appendix for *smearkase* recipe

served with strong black coffee, hot chocolate, or hot egg-nog, which Grandma and the uncles "completed" with a jig-ger of *Four Roses* bourbon from Grandma's private stash.

Long after dark, the dishes cleared and washed, left-overs packaged and divided among the aunts, we headed home. The twenty-mile trip would take a half hour. Ordi-narily, I'd fall asleep before the Chevy rounded the first turn. But not today. The thrill of Christmas will keep me awake long after I crawl into bed.

No school for more than a week. I wonder if Craig will be up for a game of "catch."....I'll give him a call...(yawn)...first thing...... tomorr........

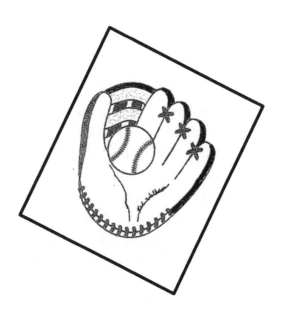

94

JOHN WAYNE

It was an ordinary day, but for some reason Momma was out of sorts. She seemed to avoid my sister Evangeline (Vangie) and me. If we asked her anything, her response was sharp and quick. She spent more time than usual just sitting in her chair – staring blankly. That wasn't like Momma. Something was on her mind. Later, that afternoon we learned the reason for her solemnity.

Aunt Olga came by and picked up our six-year-old sister, Arlene. Shortly after they left, Momma called Vangie and me into her room and motioned us to sit on the edge of the bed beside her. She sat there for quite a while, not saying a word – her eyes beginning to well. Finally she spoke up and stammered, "I'm...I'm going to have...a baby," and broke into a flood of tears.

That was exciting news! Why was she crying? I don't remember her exact words but it had to do to with the new baby being so unexpected – unplanned. I was eleven – Vangie, sixteen – Arlene, six – five years between births. Even our birth months were tightly grouped: January, March, April. We had all been planned. But this baby was an accident.

Momma's hesitant speech didn't stop there. She stammered even more when she said, "There's something else I need to tell you." With a voice filled with shame and embarrassment, in two long sentences she told us how babies are made. That must have been one of the most difficult things Momma ever had to do! And she didn't have to do it. At sixteen, Vangie must have already known far more than Momma revealed. And, I had heard the playground talk at school, although it didn't sound like what Momma said.

The baby arrived in late August. Everyone was thrilled, especially me. I finally had a brother. One simple problem remained: what are we going to call him? I wasn't involved in the deliberation. The hospital staff waited for an answer to complete the birth records. Vangie was old enough to go into the maternity ward with my folks. Obviously they had not come to a conclusion in the weeks prior. But they had determined that my brother's name would not be Germanic. I had been named Gus after my father, Gustav, and a beloved Uncle Gustav. And that decision had been made before America entered the war against Hitler and his minions. They apparently were not going to have a little Adolph or Herman tottering around the house. They needed a good American name.

"How about JOHN WAYNE," my sister quipped. "It's a good American name." Momma liked it – Daddy liked it - and that settled it. His name is JOHN (that's even Biblical) WAYNE. My parents had no idea that a popular movie star had the same name and "everybody liked him" - including my sister, who, weeks before, had watched her matinee idol star in *The Sands of Iwo Jima.*

It only took a few days for my folks to be well informed of the origin of their second son's moniker. But the hospital forms were completed and the birth record had already been logged at the county court house.

*** *** ***

Once every month the matrons of Zion Lutheran Church, (commonly called *The Ladies Aid Society)* met for conversation and coffee. The regular meetings included a monthly report on missionary efforts, church beautification, refreshments, and occasionally, words of wisdom from a guest speaker.

Momma attended the meetings as often as possible. She hadn't been for a while, but since her strength had returned after childbirth, she made the 20 mile trip once again on a sunny Tuesday afternoon, looking forward to visiting with friends and relatives. On this particular day the lecturer was none other than the pastor. Now. I'm sure that the minister of Zion, like every other small rural congregation, was kept fully informed of all the goings-on in the congregation and community – including births and babies' names.

Was it merely a coincidence that he had prepared "Choosing Your Baby's Name" as the topic for the day? The early part of his message spoke of the Scriptural mandate to "be fruitful and multiply" – and of the blessings of children (after all, he was the father of six). Eventually, he moved to the core of his discourse, a list of specifics to consider when selecting proper Christian names for children. Such as...

1. Names of parents or grandparents

2. Names of uncles, aunts and special friends are honoring

3. Avoid selecting something 'cute' from a "Book of Names"

4. Biblical names should always be considered, but don't choose blindly

5. Above all, avoid naming your children after celebrities, especially Hollywood 'stars' with questionable morals.

At the mention of item number five Momma's face flushed and she lowered her head, but felt the sting as the preacher glanced ever so briefly toward her. She desperately wanted to respond, but held her tongue and thought, *"He never said a word about John when he baptized him last Sunday!...Hummph..."Oh well, John Wayne is my last one for sure!"*

TELEVISION ARRIVES

Television came to Central Texas around 1950. In the fall of '52 our family went to the State Fair in Dallas and I was enthralled by the Hall of Science and Industry. Miniature microwave towers stretched across one large diorama in display of how various communications would be wirelessly transmitted across the nation. They were all predicting a television set in every home. *How soon would we get one?* Stations in large cities like Houston and Dallas were already broadcasting. But they were too distant to reach Andice. Austin was our only hope, and good 'ole Lady Bird Johnson came to the rescue by creating KTBC-TV. And from Temple KCEN-TV sent its signal from the opposite direction.

Since Daddy was also a Crosley appliance dealer (in addition to Maytag washing machines) he could easily get a set for us, I reasoned. However, being the first on the block was not his style. The King family, in the big red brick house on the highway, took that honor. Every once in a while my folks would accept an invitation to marvel at the King's new "wonder." They must have had a deluge of visitors in those days.

Over in Walburg things were "jumping." Uncle Norbert bought a TV for cousins Jon and Ron. Uncle Gilbert got one for his family. Even Uncle Walter splurged for Aunt Gretel and their three girls. *What do girls need a TV for?* And they all got tall-masted, motorized antennae that could be re-motely rotated to pull in signals from any direction. Although Sunday dinner and afternoons were spent mostly at Grandma Jacob's, the evenings promised an occasional hour at one of our 'up to date' relatives, watching Abbott and Costello on the Colgate Comedy Hour.

But a glimmer of hope was on the horizon. Across the street, the Catholics added a meeting room to their church property and it included a TV set - a generous gesture by the bishop to the local Mexicans, few of whom could afford such luxury. The only problem was that the room was only open Tuesday nights and Saturdays. Well, as you know, Saturday meant work in the store until late, so that left only Tuesday, if my folks would allow. They did, <u>once</u> in a while, <u>provided</u> the chores were done, the dishes were dried (my job), homework was completed, and I hadn't recently got in trouble. And it was there, surrounded by the din of Spanish gossip, that I joined the millions watching I LOVE LUCY, and for certain, they had to watch *Bishop Fulton J. Sheen*. Now, if the Mexicans could have a TV (even one shared by all) how about us?

Would you believe, one afternoon I came home, and to my surprise, in the living room stood a beautiful, 17-inch television set. (Jon and Ron had a 21-incher but, who cared?) Mine was beautiful in its gleaming, polished wood cabinet. Right outside a window a shiny antenna, on a two-inch steel pipe, rose above the roofline. And it could be aimed in any direction, but not remotely from the comfort of our couch. We had to open the window, push the screen, grab the pipe and TWIST. Oh well, beggars can't be choosers.

Cousin Oliver and his three brothers would be among the last, but eventually they too had a set. They lived with Grandma Jacob – in her house – and she was as deaf as a doorknob. You would think that fact alone would make it easy on the household – she couldn't hear Costello's scream for AAABOTTT! or The Lone Ranger's blazing guns. It wasn't the sound that set Grandma off – it was the screen – the pictures that move. Grandma was convinced that "*der Teaufel ist im haus*" (the Devil is in the house.)

Life became miserable in the Schwausch home (Grandma's home); Aunt Esther was beside herself. It didn't matter which room the set was moved to, Grandma constantly upset the applecart – even when the tube was turned off. In desperation Daddy was called. "*Gus, you've got to do something!*" But how does one argue with an elderly, deaf woman – especially your own mother?

With a pad and pen Daddy laid out his case, writing in German: the boys were young, not even teenagers – times were changing – friends all around had televisions, etc. Item by item Grandma would stubbornly reply (though deaf, she could speak very well). Finally, the argument that relieved her anxiety: Daddy explained that television, like radio many years ago, was being used to promote the Christian message, and therefore, it could not be *der Teaufel.* Grandma finally relented but on the path from her room to the kitchen she avoided the monster. Considering what television has to offer today, methinks Grandma may have been right after all.

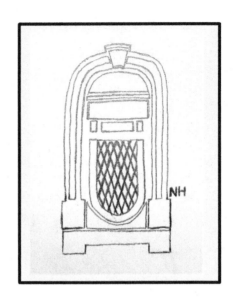

UNCLE NORBERT'S BEER JOINT

U ncle Norbert Kasparick sold beer, the hallowed beverage of the central Texas German town of Wal-burg. Homemade wine was home consumed. Hard liquor could only be sold, but not consumed, in liquor stores. So, Uncle Norbert sold beer – along with a variety of salty snacks and packets of miniature sausages.

His was not the only saloon in the town of under 120. There were two others, but KASPARICK'S was the busiest. Established by his father, acquired by Norbert, it could have passed to his first-born. That was not to be. Jon had other ambitions and the family sold the business sometime in the sixties.

However, when cousin Jon and I were preteens, no one gave a thought to two youngsters casually playing pool on the "whites only" billiard table in the main room of the joint, while the juke box bellowed country songs and Czech polka rhythms. If the "white" table was taken, we'd try the back room, the one reserved for the "coloreds." A separate nickelodeon featured "soul" artists, including Fats Domino before his discovery by "white folks." Jon would turn the volume up and we would sing along to *Maybelline* and *Blue-berry Hill* long before they became national hits.

The joint was open seven days a week - after noon on Sundays when some of the church-going folks would sit around a table, complaining about the preacher and his morning sermon. Others seeking the "hair of the dog that bit them" the night before. All to "strengthen themselves" for the week ahead.

Saturday evenings at KASPARICK'S were often raucous and particularly busy. Toward closing time many a happy patron carried a beer or two "for the road" – their empty bottles finding resting places in ditches along the way – some close to town – others farther out. Back then the empty bottles were re-filled by the suppliers – the ditch discards worth two cents each when returned, providing they landed safely – unbroken, no cracks, no chips – the source of a Sunday afternoon income for industrious waifs scouring the roadsides for castaways.

Cousin Ollie and I would hope to find at least ten good bottles. Twenty cents - all we needed to head to Uncle Norbert's and trade for a pair of big RC Colas and two bags of salty red-skinned peanuts.

You mean to say that you've never had peanuts in your Coke (or RC or Dr. Pepper)? The red-skinned ones are the best. Take a couple of big swallows to make room - pour in the nuts, slurp the head of foam as it rises up the bottle neck - (some of the skins peel away and float lazily in the liquid). Drink it slowly. With a little practice you can capture at least one nut – sometimes several - in every swig. Those were the days! Sittin' in the shade behind Ollie's smokehouse, swappin' dirty jokes and sippin' soda water.

As we gulp down the last of our hard-earned, well-deserved refreshment – shaking free a stubborn goober clinging to the bottom of the bottle - we just knew that for now "life doesn't get any better than this!"

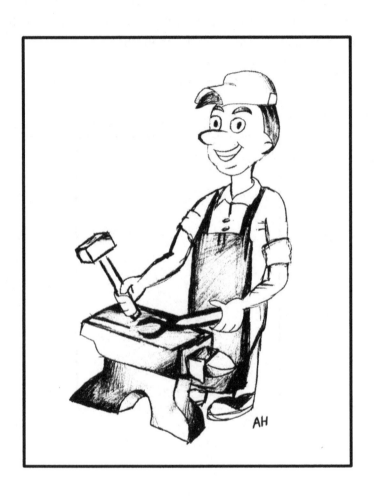

THE VILLAGES' BLACKSMITHS

> Under a spreading chestnut tree
> The village smithy stands;
> The smith, a mighty man is he,
> With large and sinewy hands;
> And the muscles of his brawny arms
> Are strong as iron bands.....

There were no chestnut trees in Andice or Walburg - or anywhere nearby. However, Longfellow's poem brings back the memories of the four blacksmiths I knew as a youth – my grandfather, two uncles, and our neighbor, Mr. Hawkins.

Grandpa Jacob was a short, rotund man – hardly over 5 feet tall, with large, strong hands – hands that still had a vise-like grip years after he no longer wielded a nine-pound hammer. I often hesitated to greet him with a handshake. He didn't realize his own residual strength. Lines of fine black soot inked the wrinkles on his knuckles and his fingernails were never completely free of the evidence of his trade.

I never saw Grandpa at the forge. He had already turned his business over to the uncles, Walter and Albert. As long as his strength would allow he would keep in touch – walking the rocky path from his house to the front doors of the shop, plopping his heavy frame on one of several old worn automobile seats, chatting with customers waiting for their plowshares, or nodding off in the warmth of the day while the monotonous "clang... clang, clang-clang" of hammer on anvil rang inside the building. And if the energy of youth in our game of "tag" invaded his sacred space or interrupted his precious tranquility he'd "shoo" us away, waving his cane mumbling in German, "Verdamten youngen!" (*Damn kids*).

.....His brow is wet with honest sweat,
He earns whate'er he can,
And looks the whole world in the face,
For he owes not any man.

When the forge was ablaze inside the shop, a constant blue haze hung in the air. The acrid smell of burnt charcoal permeated the wooden walls and timbers of the structure - a fine layer of soot settled on everything. Uncle Walter stood at the furnace, sweat dripping from the tip of his nose, staring intently at the iron, deep in the bed of charcoal, glowing white hot from the gentle breeze of the electric blower he had devised to replace the retired hand-driven bellows. Uncle Albert - busy with another contraption the two had dreamed up – an electrically driven hack saw that stopped automatically when the steel was cut through.

On a workbench near the front door sat a large wooden bucket filled with cool water drawn from the hand-dug well out back. Hanging on a nail above the bucket, was a single, worn and dented tin cup for everyone to use.

Although it had begun as a traditional blacksmith shop, my uncles turned it into much more. For years Grandpa had been the village smith, sharpening plows, "shoeing" horses, and fitting steel rims on wagon wheels.

As horses and wagons surrendered to tractors and trailers, the uncles' resourcefulness, hard work, and honesty provided a living for their two families, plus Grandma and Grandpa.

> Week in, week out from morn till night,
> You can hear his bellows blow;
> You can hear him swing his heavy sledge
> With measured beat and slow...

For me the man who seemed most like Longfellow's smith, was our neighbor, Mr. Hawkins. His small shop faced the dusty road that ran through town and passed our home. It was just at the edge of Momma's garden. Summer and winter, week in, week out – I could hear the *PING* of his hammer meeting anvil. I passed his workplace every day. I was the...

> .....children coming home from school
> Look in at the open door;
> They love to see the flaming forge,
> And hear the bellows roar.
> And watch the burning sparks that fly
> Like chaff from a threshing-floor.

Many a time I would just sit and watch as thick iron glowed reddish-white in the forge. Then with tongs and forceps the craftsman would pull the metal from the blaze and mold his creation – banging, pounding, twisting, turning - quickly, before the metal cooled - back to the blaze, glowing iron again on the anvil, curling the yielding metal around the anvil's neck. The deft with which he handled forge and flame amazed me – his tools were virtual extensions of his own hands. What had begun as a piece of iron, was now the graceful, twisted arch for a garden gate.

A man of few words – gentle, one of the kindest individuals I have ever known. I was always welcome inside his workshop. If he had a simple task to perform, he'd let me turn the crank that fanned the forge. And his eyes would say, *"Watch! See what wonders we can do."* He'd give me the hammer to flatten a piece of red-hot iron as he held it firmly with the tongs. He showed me how the edge of a plowshare is sharpened by pounding, then tempered by thrusting it into water, giving an instant hiss and a billow of steam. I'd watched him heat horseshoes and shape them on the anvil, time and again matching them to the foot of a waiting steed, and only when he was satisfied with the fit would he nail them carefully to the hoof.

> Toiling, - rejoicing, - sorrowing,
> Onward through life he goes;
> Each morning sees some task begin,
> Each evening sees it close;
> Something attempted, something done
> Has earned a night's repose

Once and only once did I make the mistake of assuming that the single thrust into the water had cooled the iron completely. Mr. Hawkins had set a flat section of metal on the concrete slab that anchored the anvil. From the hiss of the water I assumed it was cool; it looked as cool as the iron on his shelf. Carelessly, barefooted (we all went barefoot then) I walked around the anvil, and you can guess the rest.

It was a brief but important lesson about metal-working. I literally hot-footed it home for some immediate first-aid.

The art and craft of the smith is hardly known or needed today. Sadly we bid him farewell.

> Thanks, thanks to thee, my worthy friend,
> For the lesson thou has taught!
> Thus at the flaming forge of life
> Our fortunes must be wrought;
> Thus on its sounding anvil shaped
> Each burning deed and thought.

Henry Wadsworth Longfellow

116

ST ROSE OF LIMA

S t. Rose of Lima Catholic Church stood across the road from our house. I never went inside. After all, we were Lutherans and it was Catholic – Mexican Catholic at that. I do recall once, standing outside the door, risking a peek inside – the crucifix at the center - on a side pedestal, Mary, dressed in blue and white, a halo above her head. Statues! *They pray to statues in there! And the priest speaks Latin!* It wasn't a place for a good Lutheran boy to go.

But that was the inside of the church – forbidden and foreboding. Outside was quite different.

Andice, population less than 50, had no "Meskins" living in the town. They lived all around – most were sharecroppers or "renters" or just the "farm help" living in shacks, conveniently distant from the boss's house. But on Sunday they were there – their rattling pick-ups, beat-up cars and one or two wagons with mule teams parked up and down both sides of the road. Andice had more "Meskins" than "white folks" on a Sunday morning – and still even more on fiestas – Christmas, Easter, and especially the Mexican holidays of Dies y seis (September 16) and Cinco de Mayo (May 5). And celebrate they did!

Colored crepe and paper lanterns streamered the grove of trees behind the church. Pork tamales steamed from cauldrons. Over open fires, cast-iron skillets bubbled with

117

fresh frijoles and toasted hand-tossed tortillas. The men strutted in new jeans and big sombreros, while the women minded the niños and the cooking, offering sample treats to passers-by. Ancient tios (grandfathers) with gnarled hands and weathered faces sat together smoking cheap cigars and hand-rolled cigarettes, talking of days gone by. Abuelitas, ridiculed the ancient men, rocked exhausted babies and jabbered as grandmothers do, each one claiming more knowledge on the topic at hand than the other. The children played tag or hide-and-seek as music blared across the town (which wasn't much of a feat, considering Andice's size.) I wonder if the old ladies on Widder Lane got much sleep those evenings.

As anywhere, the young men eyed the señoritas - flowers in their hair - bright dresses with layers of petticoats. Every once in a while a couple would sneak off beyond the grove of trees and the glow of the paper lanterns – only to reappear some time later, pretending their dishevelment was the result of energetic dancing – but everyone knew better. And dance they all did – in true Mexican style – sombreros waving and sarapes flying – petticoats twirling, offering only a quick glimpse of leg or thigh.

In the midst of all of the eating, dancing and singing, several señoritas with large metal hoops would capture selected men, young or old, and corral them in the "jail" - a cluster of trees with a rope boundary. This was another way the church would profit from the day, since girlfriends and wives had to "bail out" their men. Some stayed incarcerated longer than they wished, while the women debated over the advisability of their release. Eventually the ransoms were paid and the bishop's purse grew a little bit heavier.

I'd walk across the road with Daddy. He'd buy a couple dozen tamales and visit with the "Meskins." He knew them all by name - even spoke a little Spanish. I was only six or seven when a señorita with a hoop "arrested" me. I had no idea of what was happening. Although she was only having fun, it wasn't fun for me. She laughed and teased in Spanish as she led me to the "jail."... Daddy quickly paid my bail.

Somewhere around midnight the music stopped – the food all gone or packed away. Everyone left with shouts of "adios" and "hasta la vista." Rattling pick-ups sputtered to life; drowsy mules clopped down the road and Andice became a quiet, little village once again.

The following day, when the church grounds were deserted, I'd return to scavenge for dropped coins and discarded treasure. Sometimes I got lucky, and the bishop's purse was short a dime or two.

TRADITION - TRADITION

A house of prayer and praise has commanded the top of same hill outside Walburg, Texas since 1882 when the congregation of Zion Lutheran Church was organized. The structure I knew as a child was positioned in true evangelical form - its main doors facing east - the two side banks of windows opening to the north and south. The six-pointed star in the round window on the bell tower may seem strange. However, while the Star of David is recognized by most as a Jewish symbol, it has been used in Christian art and architecture for centuries. A large oak tree, with branches spreading over 30 feet, grew on the front lawn and was a natural, shady spot for friends to congregate and visit after worship.

Inside, rows of benches flanked both sides of the center aisle. Above the benches a U-shaped balcony accommodated the pipe organ, choir pews and additional seating "reserved" for the high school and older youth. Only after confirmation (age 13-14) was one "certified" to sit in the balcony without an adult. Younger children sat with their parents or in separate smaller benches at the front of the nave,[5] directly under the watchful eye of *Herr Pastor*.

In true German fashion the men and boys sat on one side of the aisle - women and girls on the other. A few 'brave' men sat with their wives in the women's section, but

---

[5] Nave: The main seating area in a church

121

the opposite side was totally masculine. This separation had a practical advantage for the male of the specie. Those in the balcony were also expected to abide by the same segregation of the sexes. (But you know teenagers).

It may not have been adherence to ecclesiastical rule that determined the alignment of the edifice. Texas weather might have been a more determining factor. On the top of a hill, windows on the north and south provided better cross-ventilation than those facing east and west.

But I digress...What has this to do with the advantage for the male of the specie?

Well you see, Zion's all-male voting assembly determined that in the summertime, when the Texas sun beat through the windows on the south side, the men would sit on the north, in the shade, away from the glare and heat. Conversely, as winter came, bringing its icy 'blue northers', they would move over to the south side for the warm, welcome sunshine streaming thru its windows, reassigning the women to shiver where a constant chill poured through the drafty north wall.

Except for special occasions: weddings, funerals, Christmas programs, etc., such were the Sunday morning seating assignments as I first knew them and remained thus until I was nearing my teens, when a new minister arrived on the scene. Nothing changed immediately - then...one Sunday, eyes bulged and jaws dropped. At first there were only audible whispers - then the entire assembly began to buzz.

Youngsters in the balcony leaned over the railing to see what the commotion was all about: A flowered, broad-brimmed hat had unashamedly taken a place on the men's side of the aisle. *Rosalie was sitting with Charlie!! Won't somebody do something!?*

Was the fact that Uncle Charlie being one of the most affluent members of the congregation the reason no action was taken by the Elders? ....Hmmm...? Aunt Rosalie sat with her husband again the next Sunday, and every Sunday afterwards. One by one - Sunday after Sunday- more skirts followed suits into the male-only benches. The spell had been broken. Flowered, broad-brimmed hats blossomed everywhere.

Now, however, another serious dilemma confronted the congregational hierarchy: *Since God had created man first and then woman, it must be God's will that the men partake of the communion elements before the women.* For a while ushers made sure that the long-established ritual continued - men with their brushy mustaches, some coated with chewing tobacco residue, gulping large swigs of wine from a common chalice, leaving 'who-knows-what' behind for the ladies. Finally, a few liberated women decided they had yielded long enough and threatened to refuse the sacrament until changes were made (if not, some 'changes' just might be made at home). I need not go on.

Still, the most sacrosanct tradition of all had yet to be faced: the German language. *After all, Lutheranism was born in Germany!* From 1882 to well within the 20th century all services at Zion were conducted in the 'mother tongue'. Shortly before I was born, an English service was added - but only twice a month. Our family went to church <u>every</u> Sunday and thus, the other 'twice a months' I sat for over an hour, never understanding what was said or sung, but did appreciate the classic melodies of the hymns they boldly sang with heart and reverence.

When the new minister I mentioned earlier was 'called' to Zion, he dutifully informed the congregation that he would continue to preach in German but an English service would be included <u>every</u> Sunday. *What next! Mind you, he's going to end up doing away with German altogether. Everyone knows that God spoke German - Didn't God look for Adam and Eve in the Garden calling, "ADAM VO BIST DU?"* (Adam where are you?)

Transition came slowly. It was not only the vision of the new pastor. Many members, themselves, realized that the world around them was changing - their own children now spoke only English. The youth were dating and marrying those who didn't understand a different dialect. As feared, the importance of the old ways was fading. Eventually the German services were held only twice a month and participation diminished. Die-hard congregants attempted to erase the 'handwriting on the wall', but they knew their efforts were futile. Finally, "English-Only" became the regular worship style. To maintain a touch with the past, from time to time a retired, elderly pastor came to deliver an afternoon sermon in a 'tongue' that 'tickled the ears' of the few sitting in an almost-empty nave.

The old structure itself subsequently became too hot in summer - too cold in winter - and too small for the growing congregation. A modern worship center was planned and erected - but not before good-byes were said to a faithful 'loved one.' The new edifice needed additional space toward the front lawn. The massive oak had to go. As a hungry bulldozer chugged impatiently, the Building Committee joined hands around the trunk of the tree. Under the canopy of their 'old friend' they said their 'farewells', praising God, their *"...Help in ages past and [their] Hope for years to come."*[6]

---

[6]from 1708 hymn by Isaac Watts - based on Psalm 90

HOLDING ROPE

The tradition could only be maintained in a rural culture where roads were narrow and dusty, automobiles had no air conditioning, and large wedding receptions were held at the home of the bride. A small reception with less than one hundred guests, and the effort was hardly worthwhile. Two or three hundred and there was hope of a lucrative outcome.

All one needed was a friend and a rope long enough to stretch across the road. The object was to collect a toll from every car headed to the celebration. As festive friends neared the home it was of little consequence to pay a small toll and hurry on to the awaiting smorgasbord of beer, barbeque and all the fixin's.

It was not unusual for another pair of entrepreneurs to show up with a rope of their own and create a first toll 'gate' along the route. Heated arguments were bound to ensue as to rights to the prime toll position - usually resulting in the advantage given to either first-come-first-served or whomever was more closely related to the wedding couple.

Most drivers, in good humor and a celebratory spirit, relented at two tolls. Coins would fly from the windows initiating a scramble for 'dimes in the dust.' But a third toll rope was out of the question.

Practically everyone knew what to expect and joined in. Only an 'outsider' would be reluctant. Any hesitation on his part would be met with a tighter stretch of the rope and daring glares from determined whipper-snappers. *Won't he be surprised when he gets to the next rope up ahead!*

The money? What happened to the money? Theoretically, it was for the bride, and a presentation was occasionally made but rarely accepted. She, as well as her guests, considered it all in fun and the lads divided the spoils and pocketed their loot.

Who knows how the custom began? But those days are gone. The country roads have all been widened and paved. Receptions are rarely held at homes – large air conditioned venues with disc jockeys and dancing offer far more comfort as well as protection from the elements of Texas' unpredictable weather. It's left to become one of the historiographies that grandpas enter into – all beginning, "When I was your age...."

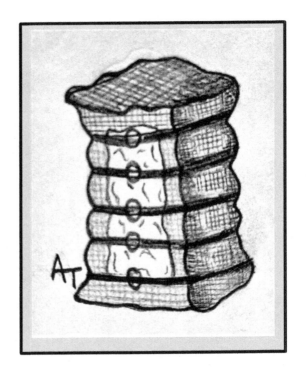

COTTON PICKIN' TIME

They called it KING COTTON. Cotton ruled the agricultural economy and everyone who depended on it. Bitter battles had been fought over it. Though some argued that the Civil War was all about states' rights, the truth lay in the fact that the movers and shakers of the Deep South needed slave labor or lose their source of wealth and power. Many of the elite, on both sides of the issue, didn't join the rank and file of the war. It was left for commoners to bleed and die. After all the dying, the great plantations disappeared but cotton was still king.

There were no plantations in Central Texas. The fields and farms had always been, for the most part, small – owned by simple people who struggled year by year to eek-out a livelihood. Cotton was their "cash crop." Unlike corn, which was food for family and livestock, one couldn't eat cotton. And the back-breaking labor in the cotton fields required determined hands to make it "pay."

By mid-summer the first of the hard, ball-shaped cotton bolls [*pronounced "bowls"*], began to open, revealing their fluffy contents – soft and snow-white, holding numerous seeds. The crop had to be gathered, but each boll, with less than half an ounce of cotton in its spiny hull, could only be retrieved by hand.

From early morning till sunset of the hot summer days, between the shade-less rows of cotton, a picker, bent to the waist, would drag a large canvas sack (some eight feet in length) plucking the bolls one by one until the sack was full and ready to be weighed and emptied – only to return to the waiting rows and filled again

If the dreaded boll weevil had not infested the plant, and the rains had come as needed, there was hope for a "bumper crop." If not, there would be "slim pickin's." Either way, it had to all be gathered – a first "easy pickin'" of the initial bolls opening, followed by a second harvest for bolls that opened later.

The Jacobs didn't raise cotton – only corn and other grain for animals. But Daddy didn't hesitate to find a way to keep us occupied part of the summer by convincing a local farmer to put up with us kids and our meager harvesting attempts. We really didn't make much of a dent in the crop, but we were out of our parents' hair. Margaret, too, recalls being "forced" to pick cotton at her granddad's farm or in the fields of a member of her father's congregation.

*** *** ***

Each summer they came – by car, by pickup and truck, in run-down school busses – every vehicle seemingly on its "last legs," but chugging along, held together with hope and bailing wire. Itinerant farm workers - entire families – seeking an honest wage, following the cotton harvest as it opened, from South Texas fields, to north across the Red River and beyond. (*"Grapes of Wrath"* in Texas).

132

They came to town inquiring of the need for pickers. Daddy would direct them to one farm or another. Hopefully, they would find temporary refuge in a single-room shack – no electricity – no running water – if lucky, there would be an outhouse. Sometimes the only solid shelter would be an empty barn. Otherwise a couple of tents or the tarp-draped, high-boarded back of a bob-tail truck would be "home." Within a few weeks they would be gone, leaving the "tailings" of the crop to the locals. Others would drift in late, only to be told to move on - the big, sad eyes of their young children standing and watching from the rear of their truck until they were out of sight – lost in the dust of the road

*** *** ***

The cotton gin at Andice was several hundred yards from our house, down the road, just across the creek. For nine months of the year it was shut and silent. When the cotton bolls opened it came to life with its noise and odor. The fields yielded their harvests. Mule-drawn wagons and trailers pulled by truck or tractor crowded the waiting lot with their loads to be ginned: cotton lint separated from its seeds and hulls - then pressed into 500 pound bales – the seeds returned to the farmer for next year's planting or sold to processing plants to be made into cattle feed, cooking oil, margarine and various creations of science and chemistry. The hulls were openly burned, sending an acrid smoke across our small town, but passing our home first, if the wind was right (or should I say "wrong").

At the height of the season the 'beast' roared continuously. Minuscule flecks of lint escaped in the separation process and drifted across the sky. And the "fires of Gehenna" with its unabated odor persisted twenty-four hours a days, seven days a week – and continued to smolder long after the operation closed in the fall.

Most of the baled cotton was hauled to the nearest railroad; its destination: Galveston, for shipment by sea to mills on the East Coast. Some, on the other hand, found their way to an empty lot near our house. Daddy had bought and kept them until he could negotiate a sale. The lot became a playground for Craig and me. We were only limited by our imagination – the rows of bales became mountain cliffs from which we fought off the bad guys in the "canyons" below – or ran in mad pursuit of each other, jumping from bale to bale or scaling their "walls" to lie at the top of our fortress, to just soak in the warmth of the late autumn sun.

THE PARTY LINE

There were no secrets on a telephone "party line." Everything was open to anyone who shared your line. The phone at Uncle Ben's home was on the line with ours. Three short rings meant the call was for us – two long rings signaled them. Vangie had no privacy if a boyfriend called. Momma could never talk freely to friends in the town. The sound of a distinct "click" was a dead giveaway that someone else had "picked up" on the call. And there were times when the "someone else" would forget she was eavesdropping and interrupt to add or correct some detail in the discussion.

When Margaret learned of her first pregnancy we were anxious to make confidential announcements to our parents. We knew, however that a call on my folks' party line would, more than likely, not be a private disclosure. It was no surprise that congratulations and well wishes were soon coming from aunts and cousins we hadn't communicated with. The "party line" had spread the word.

Sitting at her switchboard, the telephone operator was privileged to all information crossing the wires. After all, it was her responsibility to connect one party with the other and route long distance calls to the "outside," whether to Austin or Australia. With the switchboard's array of sockets, plugs and cords to unite the callers, she was a conduit of news into, around and out of town. I'd never accuse her of gossip, but there were times when items of interest spread through the community at an unusually fast pace.

My parents, however, had one advantage. Since all of our relatives spoke German, and the operator didn't, the phone conversations with kinfolks in Walburg were a mystery to the switchboard's ears.

On one particular occasion Daddy's "mother tongue" was especially useful. The store had been broken into several times. Small pilferages – cigarettes, candy bars. His prime suspects: local boys. One evening, at closing time, Daddy noticed a back door, unbarred. He was positive that it had been secured earlier that afternoon. "So that's how they got in," he thought, "they'll probably return tonight."

He didn't want to face them alone. A witness with some authority was needed, but he dare not phone the sheriff directly. The answer was simple.... A phone call to cousin Carl in Georgetown, and, conversing only in German, Daddy related his request.

The constable arrived in an unmarked vehicle. Daddy and the officer waited in the dark store near the light-switch panel until the intruders were at the cigarette shelves. A flick of a switch and four teenage knees shook in unison – a wet puddle appeared around the shoes of the younger lad.

The two were no strangers – local boys, just as he figured; their folks were regular customers in the store. It was only a short drive to their home. After a stern warning and promises made, Daddy and the constable bade everyone "good night."

Best of all, there's Daddy, the phone and his sense of humor. He liked nothing better than a good joke or a harmless prank. Jacobs Store was a small operation and had limited use of cellophane tape except for wrapping an occasional package or mending a torn dollar bill. As the rolls of adhesive diminished Daddy would phone a friend for a small supply to replenish his stock.

Before I go on, I must remind the reader that Andice was a strong Southern Baptist community, and no alcoholic beverages could be purchased anywhere within miles. Everyone knew of Daddy's German heritage and suspected that he might have a bottle of beer or two in his fridge. They could forgive him for that; it was not a heinous sin. But hard liquor was an entirely different ball game.

What puzzled the townfolks were those occasional phone calls to Billy Hoffman, at *Hoffman & Son's* in Georgetown. Billy was Daddy's source for Scotch tape, and Daddy knew, full well, that the ears at the telephone switchboard were keen to know the necessity of any long-distance call. After a few pleasantries with his fellow conspirator he would say, "By the way, Billy, can you send me another case of Scotch?" Hoffman would assure him prompt delivery, careful not to reveal the true nature of the transaction. Shortly after he retired, in a moment of reverie, Daddy told me of his deception - beyond that, he and Billy took their little ruse to their graves.

WATERMELONS

It's summer! And that meant one thing – watermelons – big juicy watermelons. The trucks would come through Andice several times each season – sometimes a long "semi-trailer" and other times only a short "bobtail." But each would be loaded with what we considered "the best" – HEMPSTEAD MELONS - the "Black Diamonds" - round dark green beauties, weighing up to thirty, forty pounds - none of the wimpy little things in stores today.

Daddy would buy ten or fifteen and mark the weight on each with a black grease pencil (they were sold by the pound) - line them all up on the store's front porch – all except one, that is. It was headed for the meat cooler in back and we knew there would be a twenty-four hour wait for our melon to totally chill. Of course, it wasn't all ours. For, as with everything else in the store, half belonged to Uncle Ben and his family.

Momma generally baked fresh bread at least once a week. And the day she baked bread was a good day for a watermelon supper. I can still imagine my father walking down the dusty road from the store to the house – our share of a Black Diamond propped on his shoulder – half of our supper on a hot summer evening – cold watermelon and fresh warm bread and butter – simple but oh, so satisfying!

Of course we devoured the whole thing (except the seeds) - and I mean the whole thing. Once the sweet, red 'flesh' was consumed, Momma didn't let the rind go to waste. The next day it was on proud display on the pantry shelf - pickled watermelon rind[7] for the winter.

THE COLT 38[8]

W hen we asked him how he got it, all my father said was, "I won it on a nickel punch board in Grandpa Doering's store."

In the first half of the 20th century, punch boards were common novelties in many stores and bars, especially in small rural towns. Most of the inexpensive boards were made of two pieces of heavy cardboard glued together with numbered 'punch-out' dime-sized circles all over the front. Hidden behind the punch circle, a paper note designated the prize. A single board could easily have as many as 200 'punch-outs'.

The customer would buy a "chance" on a five-cent 'punch', fully aware that most of the 'prize notes' said "SORRY - TRY AGAIN" - But, the board had to pay off from time to time, so once in while the "prize" was the return of the nickel investment, maybe even a dime or a quarter. (A forerunner of the scratch-off lottery).

The more lucrative boards were those that offered a chance at winning something of real value. Hundreds of boards in a particular series were made and sold to shopkeepers everywhere – BUT among all the boards there was only ONE lucky punch to win the big prize – a radio, a guitar, or even a Colt 38 revolver.

He won it on a nickel punch board. It hung, unloaded, on a nail, high in his closet. Its elevated location was enough for us kids to know our relationship to that firearm.

---

[8] Police Positive Special - Manufactured 1928

When I was ten, Daddy promised that someday it would be mine. A ten-year-old does not forget a promise like that...but daddies do.

Four years later I left home for school at Concordia in Austin. While I was there, Daddy presented the Colt to a local young man who had recently joined the Border Patrol. Since every officer had to provide his own firearm and ammunition, my generous father just <u>GAVE</u> the gun away.

"YOU PROMISED! YOU PROMISED! YOU PROMISED!" is all I could say when I discovered that <u>MY PISTOL</u> was somewhere in South Texas. I don't know how Daddy explained the situation, but in exchange for the old Colt, he purchased a new revolver for the young agent. My father was not one to let a forgotten promise go unfulfilled.

KNEEPADS

It was just a make-shift rim, nailed to a large, broad tree trunk – no backboard – no net - no pavement - just grass and a gravel driveway – but I now had my own basketball court. I loved the game – Craig, the only boy my age in town, didn't; so there was little opportunity for one-on-one competition. It was only me and my imaginary opponent:

> *Jacob's got the ball! – he's driving down court –*
> *fakes to his left – dribbles right –*
> *it's a high hook shot! – SCORE!*

It wasn't long before much of the grass wore away and disappeared; only a dirt court remained – still without a backboard. I needed something better, even if I had to nail the goal to the side of the barn. So that's what I did. Finally I had a backboard, a large white square painted on the faded red wall. Daddy wasn't too pleased. He assured me that at the end of basketball season I would have to finish painting the entire wall and eventually the rest of the barn. But he never got around to enforcing his threat. (A one-man basketball league has no end of season). Neighbors and passers-by couldn't see the net-less rim. They must have assumed the white square was waiting for some sort of rural advertising.

I created a half-court by clearing the area of rocks, weeds, and dried cow patties – then raked the ground as smooth as possible. The rocks and weeds didn't find their way back, but one had to maintain continual vigilance for reappearing patties. And a brood of chicks, following a mother hen, can totally mess up a drive to a sure two-point lay-up.

It was my most memorable Christmas gift ever. I was twelve – almost thirteen. My sister, Vangie, dug into her limited funds for a pair of basketball kneepads. WHAT A GIFT! Soft, white leather outside, with lambs-wool lining to cushion the skin – small leather belts, buckled behind the knees, kept everything snug. *I was never going to take them off.* (Well, almost never.) I wore them on the barn-yard court. I took them to school to wear over my jeans at recess with classmates in half-court scrimmages. I was the only guy in school with kneepads and proud of it! But, I dare not fall and get them scuffed or dirty and let them prove their usefulness……. WHAT A JERK!

The barn-yard court saw constant use until I left home at fourteen for school in Austin. The treasured knee-pads made the trip with me, but after their initial appearance at team "tryouts," they quickly ended up in a dark corner of my closet. Coach Lindsey wasn't going have any "hotshot" on his squad wearing something so STUPID.

High School Freshman

HIGH SCHOOL - COLLEGE

AND BEYOND

College Senior

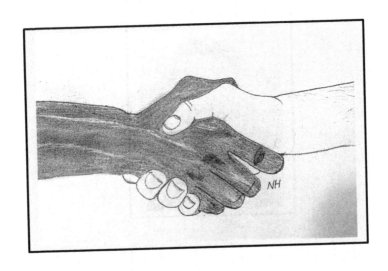

HENRY SORRELL COMES TO CONCORDIA

I came to Concordia, a scared fourteen-year-old – feigning self-confidence as my parents said 'good-bye' that warm September Sunday afternoon in 1953. It was to be my home for the next six school years – four in high school and two in junior college. The dormitory rooms were old – same original furnishings from 1926 - Old Murphy beds that swung into the closet when not in use - stuffed cotton mattresses, steam heat, no air conditioning, and three guys to a room designed to accommodate only two.

Concordia was an all-male institution, which meant that the lowly freshmen were the campus 'grunts' - expected to comply to every wish of any upperclassman, no matter how menial or inconvenient. Failure to fully submit could result in all manner of discomforts. At Concordia the practice was called 'shagging.' The supremacy of upperclassmen over the 'lower lot' was tradition in most all-male institutions, and considered by many a year-long rite of passage for the lowly 'fish.' Our only time of guaranteed refuge was in class, prescribed study hours or chapel.

In May, my freshman year, with its accompanying subservience, was finally drawing to a close. Although, next fall, as a sophomore I would still be considered an underclassman, a new slate of initiates would arrive in September, meaning, hopefully, a reprieve from some of the 'shagging' of the past nine months.

*** *** ***

The announcement at the close of a school chapel service in the spring of 1954 surprised, no shocked, everyone. The school president, Dr. George Beto, declared that the following September, Concordia's first Negro student would enroll as a freshman.

Today, such a decision wouldn't deserve or require pre-publication. But, it was 1954 and this was the South. Most of us had never even spoken to a Negro our own age, much less ever entertained the thought of sitting next to one in a classroom. However, what was of most concern was that this Negro boy was coming to Concordia – a boarding school – and it was certain that he wasn't going to get a dorm room of his own.

Beto didn't ask for volunteers. He just declared that one of us would have a "colored" roommate in the fall. Reactions were mixed. Most of the guys from the Deep South had strong racial biases and privately expressed their negative feelings. Others, reared in a more tolerant climate, were less concerned. I would be a sophomore, and it was the dean's policy to have each freshmen room with a sophomore and one upperclassman. Looking back on it, I guess that I secretly hoped that I wouldn't be one of the chosen roommates.

The following September, a skinny Negro lad arrived on the scene. He must have felt as awkward those first weeks as we did. Our misgivings of the past spring, however, soon proved to be misplaced. Henry Sorrell's assimilation into the campus routine was as quiet and peaceful as one could want.

154

HENRY JOINED THE SWIM TEAM. What a choice! Of all of the sporting events that were most likely to become an issue, it was swimming. "Coloreds" were not allowed in "white only" pools. Southerners did not swim with "blacks." But Concordia's team did, and so did anyone we competed with. It was compete or <u>we</u> forfeit.

HENRY JOINED THE FOOTBALL TEAM. His race was never questioned by any of our opponents. On one occasion, however, it did become a contentious matter for some citizens in a small town. We had traveled to their parish for the Catholic High School's homecoming game. Since the school had no lighted field of its own, they used the local public stadium for their night games. There was quite a stir when several civic-minded officials saw a black boy get off the bus and enter the locker room to suit up. In a matter of minutes we were informed that the field was not available "as long as that 'nigger' is on the property."

The local priest tried desperately to change the minds of the resolute administrators, but to no avail. Then someone mentioned that the Catholic school in a nearby town had a lighted field. Perhaps they were not using it that night. To everyone's relief, they weren't. In a short while we had all packed up – two teams, one band, cheer leaders, football referees, parents and fans – in a parade of cars and busses to a field some thirty miles away.

While the teams warmed up, everyone else pitched in to decorate the goalposts with streamers that had hastily been removed from the original field - a "homecoming" in celebration away from "home." The game started an hour late – Henry played, and even though we ended up with a 'goose-egg' on the scoreboard, that night we felt like winners.

As we headed 'home' our bus pulled up to a local drive-up hamburger stand. Coach Spitz felt like applauding our effort in spite of the loss. The man behind the window couldn't believe the order – twenty-two burgers – with fries – fifteen Cokes, six Seven-Ups, and a root beer.

HENRY JOINED THE BASKETBALL TEAM. Wherever we played he was welcome on the court, although, as a freshman, he (and us sophomores) sat on the bench until the "A" squad had run up a comfortable score.

The following spring our annual athletic awards banquet was booked at one of Austin's most popular Mexican restaurants. There would be about fifty of us. A private room was reserved, the menu selected, and a cash deposit given. We never gave it a thought to inform the restaurant that Henry would be with us. But "white" restaurants in the fifties were "white only," except those who were part of its kitchen or janitorial staff.

Well, you guessed it – El Toro told us that everything was ready and we could come in – but "NOT HIM"! We left them with their filled pots, clean plates and an empty room. Awards were handed out the following evening in the school dining hall at suppertime.

In a conversation with Henry at age eighty, he recalled the events related above and added another unforgettable incident at Concordia: A group of "locals" took umbrage to a black boy in a white school. Facing the intruders, Beto and Concordia students stood resolute in Henry's defense. When the police arrived, the disgruntled pack dissolved and walked away. After graduating from Concordia High School, Henry Sorrell served thirty-four years with the Baltimore, Maryland Police Department.[9]

An historical note: this all occurred before the forced school integrations in many parts of the South. Newspapers and television were replete with accounts of hatred and violence that swept through cities in the South as Negro children began to go to school with "whites." But against this blemished background, as far as I know, when Henry arrived, Concordia became the first integrated school in Texas, public or private.

Finally, this is not to boast of some Christian saintliness on our part. Nothing could be further from the truth. Nor did we defend his fraternity with us in an effort to join the rising tide of integration protests. It was simply because Henry was "one of us" – a schoolmate - a roommate - a teammate – a friend.

---

[9] Author's phone conversation with Henry Sorrell - October 31, 2020.

MORRIS, THE MAN AND ME

I thought I was his friend...but I wonder"

H ey, Morris!" I called, waving to the Concordia's "colored" yardman as he steered the mower along the driveway between the chapel and the library. Morris eased the vehicle to a stop. "What you been up to?" I asked. He shifted the machine into neutral and let the motor idle.

"Jus keepin' busy, Mistuh Gus. Jus keepin' busy," he replied, and took a worn kerchief from his back pocket. He wiped the sweat from his face, and a broad smile crept from behind the rag. "What you bin up to?"

"Jus keepin' busy, Mister Dunbar. Jus keepin' busy,"

Morris Dunbar and I had become friends shortly after he had arrived on the campus a few years earlier to work as the groundskeeper. Students were told only the barest details of his past - released from a Texas prison – for what offense, none of us students were quite certain. But the talk was that he had killed another black man in a fight, and, after serving several years, had been remanded to Dr. George's custody.

*** *** ***

Dr. George Beto was the president of Concordia College in Austin. Among ourselves we called him Dr. George

159

or simply Beto, but never in a derogatory manner. As head of Concordia, George Beto (pronounced Bee'-toe) had transformed a single-structure, all male, ministerial prep high school into a co-ed campus with ten buildings that accommodated both the high-school and a junior college. (The high school department has met its demise, and the college has since grown to become Concordia University Texas.)

An ordained Lutheran minister, Beto was one of the most highly respected individuals in the state, even outside the "religious community." Appointed by the governor to the Texas Prison Board in 1953, it wasn't long before the inmate population referred to him as "Walking George" or more commonly, "The Man" – a tag of respect for his six-foot-six frame, and his penetrating stare. But even more, he was known for his sense of fairness, and his belief in the dignity of every individual, including the incarcerated. In 1962 Beto left academia and assumed the post of Director of the Texas Department of Corrections. The penal reforms he initiated in the Texas prisons are world renown. A Texas prison unit bears his name and the George Beto Center for Criminal Justice at Sam Houston University was created in his honor.

*** *** ***

Morris waved his hand in a wide sweeping motion. "Da Man wants dis whole lawn dun by da end udda day," he said with a slight sigh.

"You gonna make it?" I asked.

"Hope so.......yeah, think I can," he replied – his few remaining teeth revealing the smile of a man with pride in himself and his labors.

*** *** ***

Everyone considered Morris Dunbar a diligent worker who kept to himself, and, other than in polite greetings, rarely spoke to the students at Concordia, except for a limited few.

We talked from time to time on the grounds, and once in a while I drove him home after work in one of the school's vehicles. Our conversations were never personal, and the subject of prison or his past was beyond consideration. For the most part our chats were superficial - simple exchanges of friendly pleasantries. I'd drop him off in front of his small, frame house in an all-black neighborhood on the east side of downtown Austin. He'd get out of the truck, say, "Thank ya for da ride Mistuh Gus," and walk to his door without turning back. He never invited me in – I never asked to join him.

He could have been forty-five – he could have been sixty. It's hard to guess the age of a man with a history like his. Age lines creased his face, but his body suggested a strong, younger man – the muscles in his arms glistened with sweat in the heat of the day, and when he shook your hand, you felt the power of his grip. His kind demeanor belied his past, but his eyes always held back ....something.

161

*** *** ***

We exchanged small talk for a few minutes as the tractor idled away "The Man asked me to take you home when you're done," I said, "Five o-clock ok? I'll meet you at the shed." He put the mower in gear, and revved up the engine. "Dats fine," he shouted over the din and headed out to another section of lawn.

Shortly before five I drove to the equipment barn to find him working near the open door. A garden hoe was clamped in a vise; he had a file in his hand. "You ready?" I yelled. "Jes 'bout!" he called back. "I wanna put a edge on dis ho. Gonna need it first thing Monday mornin'."

It was a Friday – end of the day, end of the week. We drove south on the Interstate – neither of us saying much, if anything. "What you doing this week-end?" I asked, trying to make small-talk.

"Nuttin….wha 'bout you?" he answered.
"Nothing special - but I'm sure looking forward to next Friday - going to Houston to see my girl."
"I didn' know yo had a gal," he said.
"We plan to get married in a couple of years - when I finish school."
"Oh….dat's good."

We drove on, only the noise of traffic disrupting the silence.

Finally, I said, "Morris, do you have a girl?" This was the first purely personal thing I had ever asked of Morris Dunbar. I just blurted it out – not thinking.

"Yeah......uh," he hesitated, "uh...no....dat is... I did....don' no mo."
"What do you mean?"
"I don' hab da money to git her wha' she wants. She dun left me – foun' some other guy."

We rounded a corner and headed toward Morris' meager home down the street. I stopped the truck. He got out and was about to say something when I interrupted.

"I wouldn't let my girl get away that easy," I joked in a "macho" sort of way. "If that were my girl I'd let her know she was mine, money or no money."

Morris peered back through the open pick-up window. He just stood there, looking directly into my eyes, as if he wanted to continue the conversation. Finally..."Thank ya for da ride Mistuh Gus." He walked away, not turning back or saying another word.

By nine o'clock Monday morning Morris had not arrived for work. Another student had gone to his home to pick him up but, returning, said no one answered the knock on the door. He assumed Morris had taken a city bus that morning. But the equipment barn was still locked and the diligent yardman was nowhere on campus.

*** *** ***

Dr. George used his spare key to enter Morris' house. A few steps inside and The Man discovered the tragic truth. Morris Dunbar was hanging from his kitchen ceiling. He had been dead since sometime Saturday.

Several blocks away the Austin police found the body of a middle-aged black woman on the floor of her bedroom - strangled. I don't remember what name the newspaper gave - just something about Morris Dunbar and the words "estranged girlfriend."

*** *** ***

It's been over fifty years. To this date, only a few have heard the story of the last conversation between Morris and me. I wouldn't have dared tell The Man. Was I partly to blame? Did I, unknowingly, prompt a simple, uneducated man, hurting over his lost love, to murder and suicide? I had been joking! Careless words - unintended consequences.

I thought I was his friend, but I wonder...

March 1, 2009

AT THE FEET OF GENIUS....

An expression befitting those of us who had the privilege of attending Concordia, especially as high school students. The academic level of our school was enviable, to say the least.

Concordia had been founded as a preparatory academy for future pastors and teachers in Lutheran churches and schools. Although it opened in 1926 as a high school, it was always known as Concordia College. Though small, its instructional staff was filled with respected scholars. When it grew to include a Junior College, an accredited college faculty was required. In addition to the substantial ministerial training of many of its instructors, most had advanced degrees in secular subjects – math, science, literature, languages, music, etc. Few high school students in the state could claim a more comprehensive source of scholarship – a college faculty responsible for the enlightenment of simple fourteen-year-old high school freshmen.

Out of respect (or convention) we all referred to our instructors as *Professor* or '*Prof*'. As you can imagine, such "gathering of genius" was bound to spawn its own circle of individualists. None were more different from each other than professors Viehweg and Huebschmann.

*** *** ***

By 1954 Gotthold Viehweg was nearing the end of his teaching career. With German as his mother-tongue, he mastered Latin and Greek before coming to America in 1914, serving as an itinerant circuit-riding pastor to scattered German-speaking communities in America's mid-west. Short in stature but tall in humility, Viehweg was always neatly dressed, soft-spoken and predictable – very predictable.

My pastor had studied under Professor Viehweg when he had attended Concordia as a boy. Before I left for school he took me aside and said:

"Let me tell you about Professor Viehweg. In 1928 he was my instructor. And in every class – I mean every class, he would come into the room – take off his coat and methodically drape it across a chair – take his seat and remove his pocket watch, which he placed on the desk and carefully wound the lengthy chain around it. After retrieving a dictionary from a drawer, he positioned it squarely on his desk and inclined his worn text against the dictionary's spine – then, making one last seat-adjusting shift, he would declare in his deep accented voice, 'LET US BEGIN.'"

Twenty-seven years later we awaited his entry for our first German class. The elderly professor came into the room and - exactly as my pastor had described, he repeated the ritual, not one effect different.

We loved the old man, even though his assignments were challenging and his insistence on precise pronunciation was frustrating to some.

He loved music, especially the songs of his homeland. Thus, from time to time we were able to persuade him to set the books aside and find an empty music room. There he would take command of the piano and introduce us to various German lieder. We sang along with gusto.

*** *** ***

Professor Eugene Huebschmann was the lone faculty member of the school's science department and, being a physicist you can guess, a world apart (maybe two worlds) from Prof. Viehweg. Huebschmann was the personification of the eccentric scientist – no tie, wrinkled shirt and several separated whisks of hair, all askew, on top of his balding head.

We knew little of his academic background, but his off-hour and summer "escapades" were intriguing. He spent many evenings and weekends in various laboratories at the University of Texas. Previous summers he had been in New Mexico at the atomic proving grounds. One fall he began his class by telling us, "Remember this name – Wernher von Braun. He will soon be famous." Von Braun was one of America's premier scientists, responsible for development of NASA rockets. Huebschmann became a friend and colleague of von Braun and had worked with him that summer. A year later he spent the summer at Cape Canaveral (now

Cape Kennedy) designing "launch windows" for test rockets. All of this occurred before Russia sent "Sputnik" into space. Americans had not even heard the word *astronaut*.

In his classroom Prof Huebschmann was constantly in motion – a whirlwind, physically and verbally. His most remembered phrase was, "Eeekles, eekle to eekles are eekle." On the board he wrote $(===) = (===)$ are $=$ (equals equal to equals are equal), basic, but unforgettable. Waving one finger high in the air, he would go deeper into theory than we understood, or were ever required to grasp, but he would expound nevertheless.

Prior to the fall of 1955 Concordia had been an all-male institution. In September, the first group of girls, fresh out of high school, sat smiling awaiting their initial college lecture by none other than (you guessed it) Professor Huebschmann. No one had informed the ladies of the prof's idiosyncrasies. Fifty minutes later, the class dismissal bell found twenty hysteric females pouring from the room, tears streaking their make-up, crying "We'll never make it! "We'll never graduate!" Professor Huebschmann had pontificated beyond belief.

Everyone knew that Professors Viehweg and Huebschmann were not the best of friends – they only spoke to one another when necessary and took separate sidewalks from their offices to the classroom building. Worlds apart, I said above, but in one fortuitous way, they were very close.

It just happened (or perhaps assigned by someone "above their grade") that the two "warriors" once shared a wall between their classrooms – the very wall on which hung each of their respective blackboards, back to back. (No white-boards or digital screens back then.) I assure the reader that the following actually happened.

In his usual manner, Professor Huebschmann began with some hypothesis that we knew was going to become complicated. Invariably he would resort to the chalkboard for emphasis. As expected, his illustration became quite lengthy, detailed and energized – pieces of chalk flying from his hand as they broke against the slate. In the midst of his enthusiasm, the classroom door suddenly opened. At the portal stood a small but determined Professor Viehweg, hands straight at his side. He took one stiff military step forward, eyes locked on his nemesis. "Professor Huebschmann!" he declared, his German accent deep and authoritarian, "Ve don't mind eff you write on der chalkboard! BUT! PLEEZE!.... DON'T ENGRRAVE!" A quick step backward, an about-face and the door went SLAM! Huebschmann saluted the closed door and resumed his lecture, but with a little less enthusiasm.

In closing, it was not my intention to ignore the other respected mentors at Concordia: Dinda: Latin – Leja: literature – Olsen: music – Beto: friend - to name a few. It is simply that the two I have recounted at length were so unique and colorful. How blessed I was to be *Sitting at the Feet of Genius,* or should I say *Standing on the Shoulders of Giants.*

MISSING ELVIS

In March of 1958 America's most famous movie and music star was drafted into the United States Army and sent to Fort Hood for basic training. (Approximately 30 miles from Andice.) Millions of teen-age girls were devastated. One young lady was thrilled, however. Not only for the fact that Fort Hood adjoined her home town of Killeen, but, as luck would have it, Elvis rented the house next door. Although Presley was barracked with other draftees, he needed a place where, when he had leave of the post, he could meet with business managers, musicians, and whoever might be required to drive his entertainment empire.

I don't recall the girl's name, I only met her on this one occasion. For the sake of convenience in this account I'll call her "Kit." In the weeks between March and September, Kit claimed to have visited the renowned rock star in his "home". Although she lived in Killeen, she would come to Andice with her minister father, who served as interim pastor of the local Baptist Church. Kit and my cousin had become friends. She had repeatedly offered to take Katherine to meet her famous "neighbor," but they never settled on a time.

The army pushed the two girls into action. Elvis was to be transferred overseas to Germany. There was one last chance. Katherine and I were both home from school that last Friday in September. Kit was in Andice too. "Come on, let's all go," she said, "he's due to leave tomorrow." My fourteen-year old sister, Arlene, was determined to tag along.

Momma was reluctant, not just for Arlene, but for all of us. It would soon be dark and it was threatening rain. Most of the 25 mile trip from Andice to Killeen was a narrow highway, notorious for its record of weekend inebriated drivers.

After thirty minutes Momma relented and the four of us – Kit, Katherine, Arlene and I – were on our way. We knew it was Elvis' last night at the Killeen home, but Kit was sure that he would invite us in, if only for a few minutes.

Driving as fast as I dared in the rain and dark, we finally pulled into Kit's driveway, and ran through a downpour to the house next door. But Elvis didn't greet us. It was an associate.

"He's gone," he said, his words almost as hollow as if Elvis had died. "He went back to the barracks half-hour ago. They leave before daylight tomorrow. Sorry, kids, you just missed him."

Elvis is now gone forever. His songs still sell in the millions. His movies reappear on television every year in January, his birth month and August, the month he died.

"Elvis impersonators" draw sold-out crowds that continue to cheer when the announcer says, "Ladies and

Gentlemen! Elvis has left the building." (An announcer's common closing of his personal performances). It's amazing that, years after his death, so many fans are still...... missing Elvis.

OFF TO YANKEE-LAND

In September, 1959, three of us were off to college in the environs of the cold North. My cousins Katherine, Lawrence and I were headed farther from home than we had ever been – Lawrence for seminary studies in Ft. Wayne, Indiana – Katherine and I would end up at Concordia Teachers College in River Forest, Illinois. Trunks filled with clothes and other dorm necessities had been shipped ahead.

It would take well over 24 hours to make the trip - no freeways or tollways to whisk us along – and the maximum speed limit on the best of roads was 60. In Lawrence's car, two in the front, the back seat for one of us to stretch out, we left Texas on a hot September day, facing over ten hours of summer heat before sundown and the hope of cooler traveling. Then a nighttime of unfamiliar and poorly marked roads through Arkansas, Missouri, and part of Illinois, before daylight.

Refueling was a serious problem: In the "fifties" there were almost no 24-hour service stations. Most closed around ten – if lucky, we might find one open until twelve. No convenience stores with gas pumps – certainly nothing like BUCKEE'S. But we were determined to drive all night, aware of the scant possibility of gassing-up between midnight and dawn. That meant watching the gauge carefully, and taking advantage of any open stations, even if we had filled the tank and emptied our bladders only an hour before.

By mid-afternoon the next day we turned onto the seminary drive – tired and hungry. All we had eaten as we drove were sandwiches our mothers had prepared and bags of chips and peanuts we were able to grab along the way.

From Ft. Wayne, Katherine and I boarded the train for the short trip to Chicago. Grand Central Station in the nation's third largest city was an imposing edifice, especially for two 'hay-seeds' who had never experienced anything larger than a Greyhound Bus Station. Now we had to run the gauntlet of the crowd and the city's busy streets for the last leg of our pilgrimage.

Carrying all our baggage, we managed to lug them up the steps of an elevated train platform, hoping to catch the one heading west to the very end of the line in River Forest. Had we hopped the wrong train we could have ended up along Lake Michigan's shore or south at Chicago's famous stock yards and slums. But we made it, found a pay phone, called the school to send a shuttle, and finally, phoned home to assure anxious parents that their "babies" were safe and sound.

LUTHERBROOK

It was autumn 1960 at Concordia Teachers College, River Forest, (now Concordia University Chicago). I had driven my new Ford Falcon station wagon from Texas to Illinois, hoping to find a part time job. Only seniors were permitted to have automobiles, and garaging them would be our own responsibility. As a resident-student my car was not allowed on campus, and the local ordinance prohibiting overnight on-street parking was strictly enforced. Fortunately, the previous June, I had reserved a space in the garage of a local homeowner.

Ten miles from my dorm, Lutherbrook Children's Home in Addison needed a week-end supervisor to organize and monitor various activities for a dozen or more of the older girls and boys - Saturdays 9-5, lunch included, and Sunday afternoons.

The Lutherbrook edifice was an ugly gray, multi-story, stone structure with two residential wings separated by a central administration and activities area. Years before it was the previous site of the institution from which I had just driven, Concordia Teachers College. As a matter of fact, the original college building, a single-room log cabin, built in 1864, still stood behind the stone edifice, but now the old log house only served as the final resting place for items too useless to keep but too "valuable" to get rid of.

With a confident stride I entered the office of the Home's director, Mr. Robert Schlesselman. (Mr. S.) He knew I was in my final year at the same institution from which he had graduated over 15 years before. I don't recall much of the interview, but he opened with, "Well, Gus, where are you from?"

Assuming he knew little or cared less of Texas geography, I replied "I was born and raised in a spot not far from Austin." (Close enough, I thought. At least this Yankee might know the state's capital city.)

"How far?" he asked.

"A few miles from Georgetown," I replied – (Maybe he had heard of our county seat.)

"Where exactly?" he probed.

"It's a little place called Andice, but my home church is in Walburg."

"I know Walburg." He smiled. (I blinked). He continued, "I spent my first teaching years in Houston and Austin. I've been to Walburg numerous times. You ever heard of…" and he listed the names of several well-known Lutheran pastors and teachers in central Texas. "Drank Walburg beer with most of them!"

Who would've known? I got the job. And what a job! The older children, ranged from age 12-16. The younger ones were between the ages of 8-12. Most had been neglected, abused or abandoned. Some had been placed in Lutherbook by court order as protection from the physical and/or emotional trauma they had endured in their homes.

For the first few months, Saturday and Sunday afternoons was dodgeball, volleyball, softball, field hockey, croquet, etc. You name it, we played it! Then winter arrived and someone suggested we go ice-skating on the pond in the nearby park. The Home had skates for the kids, and luckily, there were none large enough for me...until they found an ancient pair of stiff, black leather skates in the old log cabin – They looked like their previous owners were the original 1864 students. But the blades were still attached and some burlap twine replaced the rotten laces. We headed to the park, a half-dozen kids and me, in the Home's big station wagon.

Everyone put on their skates and the youngsters quickly glided off on the pond, leaving me sitting (very happily I must say) in the snow on the edge of the pond, staring at the two precarious, thin blades on the bottom of my feet. "Come on, Mr. Jacob!" they cried. I never learned who, but someone shouted, "Chicken!"

That did it! No Texan is going to let that pass. I struggled to stand; then wobbled several yards onto the ice. I could hear snickers in the distance. Did they know something I didn't? How thick does this ice have to be? I could see fish swimming beneath my feet!

OK. So far it's supporting my weight, but what if I fall? Will it hold if 180 pounds comes crashing down? It held. Somehow I managed to "skate" (if you can call it that) to the center of the pond. But, OH MY ACHING ANKLES! There's only one way that I was going to make it back. Swallowing my pride, on hands and knees I crawled to the safety of the pond's bank, leaving a half dozen kids laughing hysterically. Next time, I vowed I'd do better. And I did. Not much better, but they no longer laughed <u>at</u> me but <u>with</u> me, even though I could never keep up.

And what a job it became!

One afternoon, Mr. S. called me to his office. The houseparent for the older boys had taken a leave of absence. Mr. S. asked if I would consider the position until the end of the school year. It would mean supervising the boys every day after school, helping with their homework, and daily chronicling their demeanor and behavior in individual diaries kept by the Home on each of them. (The diary entries would later be reviewed by a psychologist.) My Saturday and Sunday responsibilities with both the boys and the girls would continue. There would be a small increase in salary, all meals with the staff and a private room and bath.

It was my final semester of school with a light scholastic load – three subjects, as I recall. The offer was too good to pass up and would save the expense of campus housing and meals. After ten each night my time was my own to study or relax, providing there were no interruptions from "my boys."

Charlie[10] was a handsome young lad. In June he would turn sixteen and leave the Home. But the future did not look promising. Anger continued to rage within. He rarely joined the others in games. If he did, he often found ways to disrupt. Once he had purloined a knife from the kitchen and threatened to use it - not on others, but himself. Although alarms would sound if doors opened at night, Charlie found ways to sneak away and wander aimlessly around the grounds after midnight - searching - and for what? He didn't know.

There was Sven – gentle, meek. He was fourteen and so much wanting and needing to be a man. Not for the sake of his own ego, but for Ingrid, his little sister in another wing on the far side of the building - the wing for the younger girls at the Home. Abuse had not been the reason for the two being here – it was love – the love of their parents, both of whom were deaf. They lived in a remote part of the Midwest, unable in their silent world to provide for their dearest treasures.

Although Sven and Ingrid ate at separate tables, each with their own age group, they exchanged glances and "talked" across the room in the sign language they learned from birth. Or they simply touched fingers as they passed in the hall, using every opportunity to enforce the inseparable bond between them. Every morning the two would stroll hand-in-hand to the Lutheran school across the street. He

---

[10] The actual names of all children mentioned in this chapter have been changed

185

was tall for his age and she was just a little thing. At the sound of the closing bell, one would wait for the other so they could walk back to the Home together, only then to resume their separate lives.

Nighttime: the time when fears assail and tears emerge, not only for many adults, but also for children, especially those who have known little love.

I didn't expect the soft whimpering I heard as I peeked in after midnight on my first day as a houseparent. It wasn't the weeping of a child unable to rest, but the low sobs of a sleeping fifteen-year-old in unconscious emotional pain

Bold and brash, Matt was one of the oldest of his group. You couldn't make him cry! He was dark – not his skin – but his countenance, his...look, enhanced by his jet black hair and his deep, penetrating eyes, that seemed to look, not at you, but through you. Almost everything about him seemed sinister – almost ...*evil.* Entries in Matt's diary by others confirmed that I was not alone in my assessment. How do you reach a boy who doesn't want to be reached – one whom roommates and even some adults fear?

The older girls joined 'my boys' in the weekend pursuits. Most memorable was Claire, a pretty young thing – lovely in face and form. Some would say that she was "15 going on 20." And she knew it – vibrant and flirtatious. Warnings not to be alone with her were taken seriously by all male staff members - she was "experienced" beyond her years, especially for a girl in 1961. The other girls her age disliked her, and for the most part shut her out – but true friendships among the children of Lutherbrook were rare if not completely non-existent. They all carried "baggage" that they would not share and that others would not touch. I was told that Claire had been repeatedly raped by her step-father and she had made a serious attempt to kill him and herself. Her wounds were deep - evidenced by her unpredictable and frequent mood swings. I doubt if she had ever known anyone who loved her, even her own mother. But she could easily catch the eye of any young unsuspecting male.

Finally, there was Anthony. Everyone called him Tony, and although he wasn't in my charge, he never failed to greet me with a smile. Tony was the most gregarious kid in the entire home. Proud of his Italian heritage, the nine-year-old commanded attention from all the girls, even the teen-agers - especially Claire. Tony was both a charm and a charmer, without a care in the world – or so it seemed.

One afternoon I was startled by screams from the ward down the hall. It was Tony - not only was he screaming but from his mouth came the most foul language imaginable. Opening the door, I saw his housemother, a quiet middle-aged woman, sitting patiently on a chair near the window. Tony stood, yelling out the window, invectives streaming from his lungs at something far away. Then he turned, and with the same intensity unloaded his rage at the woman – calling her every vulgar name he knew – and I mean every name and every vulgar word. She just sat there, saying nothing, but loving him with her eyes. I closed the door and went about my day – leaving Tony to his raging. But why? Why, from this adorable child?

It was Sunday – not just any Sunday - it was the first Sunday of the month – visiting day. With the approval of the court, parents could spend several hours in the afternoon with their children – some could even take off-campus outings. A few parents of the younger children came – hardly any came for the older ones. For hours Tony had stood quietly looking out of the second-story window, just as he did every first Sunday of the month.

He had been watching as 'good-byes' were being said. And he knew that _they_ were not coming today. _They_ didn't come last month, or the month before. Some parents came once in a while – but not his. *THEY NEVER CAME.* Not once in the two years that he had been at Lutherbrook. The unwanted little nine- year- old could not contain his anger…his grief…his despair. In spite of all the love that his housemother tried to give, he did not want _her_ love – *HE WANTED THEIR LOVE.* Would they ever come? Or like many of the older children would his heart eventually harden to the reality of his tragic existence?

GRADUATION, 1961 - I had earned my degree, and would soon return home, get married, and begin teaching grades five and six at a Lutheran school in Houston. My parents with Margaret, my fiancé, had come from Texas to celebrate. Mr. S. provided rooms at Lutherbrook for their stay.

My last few moments at Lutherbrook would become an indelible memory, more fixed than I could ever have imagined. As we packed our cars to leave, parents were arriving, and children were running to greet them. It was another Sunday afternoon – the first Sunday of the month. I paused to look back one more time at the ugly, old, gray building. My gaze turned to a second-floor window where a little boy stood watching …waiting …hoping… …maybe today.

WINNING MARGARET'S HAND

Pasadena, Texas – Sunday July 9, 1961 – the forecast is rain – lots of rain – and rain it did – streets were flooded by early afternoon and we still had to hold a brief rehearsal, show my parents our apartment and get back in time to change into tuxes and dresses. Oh, by the way, this is the day Margaret Bielefeldt and I will pledge our vows of love and faithfulness to each other.

Long ago, at another time and place, our lives came together. Her family had moved to Walburg, where her father served as the pastor of Zion Lutheran. She was a scrawny nine-year-old and I was ten. We had little to do with each other until ages twelve and thirteen, when we were in school together.[11] She was still a skinny kid and she considered me a jerk. And that's much the way it remained until we were both in high school.

I'll try to make this as un-complicated as I can. I attended Concordia in Austin, a boarding school with boys from all parts of the country.

Chuck, Sam and I were classmates. Chuck was my roommate - Sam is Margaret's cousin. Chuck had accompanied Sam on several weekend visits to Margaret's family and

---

[11] After six years at Andice School, I attended Zion's school in Walburg for two years - grades 7 & 8.

191

things had begun to "spark" between the two. But the school year was drawing to a close and in a few weeks Chuck would be back home in Boston - and he was worried. Margaret had previously gone with other local boys. And there was a whole summer of fun ahead. Chuck knew that Margaret didn't care much for me.

Finally he said, "Gus, would you...I mean...?"

I knew exactly what he meant. "Don't worry," I replied, "you can count on me."

It's true that the relationship between Margaret and me had always been on the cool side. Not a lot had changed over the years. But one Sunday, after church, I couldn't take my eyes off this cute young thing with short bobbed hair and a winsome smile – She's not the same scrawny kid I once knew – this one's "pretty and petite."

"Why not," I thought, "Would she?"... She did! The next weekend we had our first date and a couple more before summer ended.

What was I going to say to Chuck? This was never my intention. What kind of friend would he think I am?

In September we returned to school for our senior year. Needless to say, Chuck and I didn't room together this time. He did go to see her one more time, in a valiant attempt to "rekindle the flame." After graduation, Boston became his permanent home.

Soon after, Margaret and her family moved to Pasadena, Texas, and our courtship continued for the next five years. I was able to find summer work in nearby industries and we were together most every evening, unless I was scheduled for the night shift. Then came the two years of extended absences as my final college studies took me to Illinois. Phone calls were rare. Letters had to suffice.

Practically five years from our first date we stood at the altar. Her father performed the ceremony. If it weren't for our wedding photos, I couldn't tell you much about who was there or what happened – EXCEPT for one most unusual incident: The vows were done, the prayers were said, the blessing was given, the kiss was as long as propriety allowed. I turned with my bride and we marched arm-in-arm up the aisle – unaware that her father, clerical robe and all, was right behind us stride for stride.

In the tiny lobby of the church I only got a moment to embrace and kiss my beautiful bride again when "Dad" stepped between us to give his daughter a quick hug. Then, to my surprise, I felt his lips on mine – a brief, wet kiss - brief, but totally unexpected. What had prompted a staunch conservative minister to take such bold liberty?

I've always maintained that it was an unrestrained relief at having finally married off the first of his seven progeny. I'll never know. To his dying day Dad continued to insist that the episode never happened.

PERSONAL MUSINGS

BIMM – BOMM (REPRISE)

Where have all the church bells gone?
I don't hear them any more.

Today, as modern houses of worship are constructed, bells are hardly a consideration. In older edifices they hang mute and forgotten. There was once a time when, throughout our land, bells rang out every Sunday morning – from huge cathedral spires in crowded cities - to the simple belfries of remote rural chapels. Many have been silenced by noise ordinances – but most by apathy and inconvenience.

In years past, the peal of church bells served more than a call to worship. They tolled in trying times, signaling emergencies and news of utmost importance. The clanging of the bells raised the alarm of fire in the town – accident at the mill – mishap in the mine. They cried for help to all able bodied.

Few listened to the radio on Sundays in 1941. Old folks recall that December afternoon. Most were home from church, enjoying a welcome nap, reading the Sunday paper or playing a friendly game of horseshoes with friends when bells rang all over town, interrupting their leisure. Churches in the countryside joined in the harrowing announcement: The Japanese had attacked America at Pearl Harbor. All over our nation bells were the harbingers of a national crisis – a call to arms. During the conflict that followed, in many

197

localities bells fell silent, in respect of those who were fighting.

Finally, after years of war, they rang again - not in alarm, but in victory – loud, long and clear.

*** *** ***

My home was over twenty miles from church. Only on rare occasions did I hear Zion's bells other than for worship. Once, however, when visiting a cousin on a Saturday, the bells rang out, sharp and distinct. "They do that every Saturday." I was told. On a calm day, in the quiet of rural central Texas, the bells could be heard from miles away. Their chiming at sunset called to everyone: "Prepare your hearts. Another week has passed…. A day of rest is at hand; the morrow is sacred."

*** *** ***

On another occasion, at my sister's farm one mid-week morning, off in the distance came the faint but familiar "bimm – bomm" from Zion's steeple. They rang for some time - then suddenly stopped. A single bell began to toll a sad announcement that someone had died. The chiming of both bells garnered everyone's attention. The lone bell sounded the age of the deceased – one peal for each year. In the tightly knit German community everyone knew everyone – their ages – their ailments. They would count the tolls. Seventy-eight: Grandpa Braun, he's been ill a long time -- Eighty-nine: that's got to be Widow Schmidt. - Three – only three? Oh! No! Someone's child!

In a few days the sequence is repeated. As mourn-
ers make their way from church to graveside, both bells
ring their dual cadence - a brief pause - once again the solitary bell tolls the years - a serious reminder to "number our
days."

*** *** ***

The fond memories of bells at seasons of celebration
are unforgettable. Little can compare to their melody at
Christmas – the proclamation that God is with us - resonating
a song of "Peace on Earth," - the same peace that angels
brought to shepherds long-ago. A few months later they ring
the Easter shout of resurrection.

I miss the bells, especially the memory of New
Year's Eves as a teenager. – ringing out the old year, ringing
in the new. Following a brief service in church, the "old
folks" went off to private gatherings or home to the comfort
of their beds. The youth, however, stayed - first to "party"
in the school gymnasium - later to "watch" the passing of
"the hour."

In the cold December night, under the light of moon
and stars, we stood at the base of the steeple counting the
minutes as the New Year approached. At the stroke of
twelve, the heavy bells resonated through the nighttime air.
The neighboring pair down the road at St. Peter's applauded
the event, while, from the opposite direction and several hills
beyond, the bells of St. Mary's joined in the jubilation. And,
if you were fortunate enough to be with someone special,

199

you never even felt the chill of midnight as you pulled her close and kissed her quickly – very quickly.

I miss the bells. I suppose, if they were never a part of your life, it would be difficult to share in my reverie. Bells have played such an important part in the lives of individuals and communities throughout history. Even a cracked and muted bell has its place of honor in Philadelphia.

I miss the bells. Our culture's cacophony has not just muffled their message. It has silenced most of them completely, hiding sweet symphonies from generations yet unborn. I would dread to be awakened by a call to arms or announcement of disaster. However, at times I need the dirge reminder that one day it will be me 'for whom the bell tolls.' But, for now I will be grateful for my remaining years….and, on cold December eves I'll close my eyes, listen for the long-ago "bimm-bomm" celebration and cherish the memory of a stolen kiss at midnight.

GOD'S FAITHFULNESS

The following narratives must be told. They are not
expressions of the limit of God's faithfulness,
but continual reminders that He is,
has been and forever will be
FAITHFUL.

DECEMBER 10, 1966

I am alone in our house in Port Arthur, Texas. Today
Margaret gave birth to a third beautiful daughter, and
I'm depressed. Maybe that's not the word I want – 'des-
perate' is more accurate – feeling the weight of the world on
my shoulders. I have a wife and now three children to support, doctor and medical bills to pay, charges at Howard's
Grocery and we have less than four dollars in the bank. What
am I to do?

Our two older girls are staying with friends while
Margaret remains in the hospital. She and the baby are both
doing well. I had hoped it would be a boy, but after one look
at that precious, little face, all necessity for a male to carry
my name vanished. What a joy! But what am I to do?

I don't recall how long I paced the floor. I do recall
walking to our room and falling face down on our bed. With
heaving sobs I cried… *How, God? How am I to care for my
wife and these beautiful children you have given me? God,
I'm afraid! How? How? How?*

My prayer became jumbled thoughts and emotions that words could not express. How long I lay there – how long I prayed – I do not know. It may have been minutes – it may have been hours. I awoke, yet I know that I had not slept. It was like a gentle hand was on my shoulder. My mind was calm. My fear was gone. Joy! Only joy and a certainty that all is well. I went back to the hospital to kiss my wife and hold my baby girl.

The following month an official-looking letter arrived in the mail. It was from the U.S. Department of Education. What in the world?

I had been accepted as one of fifty teachers in the U.S. to participate in a six-week summer seminar on dyslexia among elementary school children – at Lamar University in Beaumont – just 15 miles away. In addition to all expenses being paid – tuition, fees, books, etc. A housing stipend and a per diem for food was also included. Since we lived so close, there was no reimbursement for travel, but housing and food allowances were automatic. And to top it all off, at the end of the session, there would be no exams, and I would earn nine hours of academic credit toward my masters program – over one-fourth of the total hours required.

I had completely forgotten! It was over six months earlier that I had applied, but never gave it another thought. Only 50 individuals from all over the U.S. – not a chance! But now, I was to be one of the two private school educators selected for the program.

In late May the first check for $400 arrived and in mid-July another $400. Eight hundred dollars – more than a month's salary - and college credit. I don't know when you might be reading this, but it was a time when one could buy a brand new, fully loaded Oldsmobile for $3,000. What a blessing! The hand that had rested on my heaving shoulders became two strong arms wrapped lovingly around me.

Fear not I am with thee, oh be not dismayed.
For I am thy God, and will still give thee aid.
I'll strengthen thee, help thee, and cause thee to stand
Upheld by my righteous, omnipotent hand.[12]

SUMMER, 1968

"Your little girl is very sick," he told us. *"We're do-ing all we can,.. but..."* We didn't want to hear what would follow that *"BUT"*... He stopped there, we saw the look in his eyes.

She was only 20 months old.

It all began earlier that afternoon. I had come home, after packing some personal items still left in my school classroom. I had accepted an offer to head a Lutheran school in Houston and was putting things in order, completing my obligations to Trinity School, Port Arthur.

Margaret met me at the door, almost frantic. Camille

---

[12] 19th Century hymn verse based on Isaiah 41:10

(we called her Cammy) had not been feeling well when I left that morning. Now, she had a raging fever and severe diarrhea. Hopefully, our doctor was in. He was, but immediately told us to get to the hospital. He would follow.

Not certain of the nature of her illness, or what antibiotics and course of treatment to pursue, Dr. Ross made an educated guess regarding initial action. Cammy's blood tests indicated a desperately high level of white blood cells. We learned later that some considered the level fatally high. An extreme strep infection. That's what the "but" was all about.

There was no pediatric ward in the small hospital. She was placed in a regular room - ice packs around her little body. Margaret and I stayed with her – nurses checked her regularly. Her weak cries of *"Mommy, I'm cold – I'm thirsty,"* were heartbreaking. There was little we could do but pray and quietly assure her that we were there.

A nurse came to check. One brief glance, a look of panic in her eyes - she quickly spun around and rushed from the room. Back again with another nurse and a doctor. They hurried us out and shut the door. What did it mean? Our hearts sank – we knew what it meant. We might walk back into that room and our little one would be gone.

She was so young. Her bubbling disposition – her bright smile had completely erased any wish I might have had for her to have been a boy. While our phonograph played *Dance, Gal, Gimme the Banjo,* she would hop and spin around the room. She would giggle happily as her two big sisters pushed her down the sidewalk in her stroller.

Cammy had been such a blessing, tripling the joy of parenthood. *Not now, Lord, not now! What are they doing in that room? Why is it taking so long?* The expression on the doctor's face was one we did not want to see. *"You can see her now,"* he said, leading us back to the room. *"She's struggling. You must realize that your little girl is very sick. We're doing all we can...but..."* He bit his lower lip, then turned and walked away.

Margaret and I held each other, sat and prayed together – finding it ever so difficult to put our anguish into words. Of course I prayed," *Thy will be done."* Isn't that what Christians are supposed to say at a time like this? But did I mean it? Deep in my being, did I really mean it? Strangely, somewhere in the midst of all my pleadings, I found myself saying,

"Thank you, Lord. Thank you for bringing such joy into our lives. Over a year and a half of blessing! If this was your purpose in giving her to us, then that purpose has been fulfilled. After all, Lord, she never really was ours in the first place. She's yours – she always has been – a gift to us for a season. If that season is over and the work you sent her to do – to gladden the hearts of a young family – if that task has been accomplished, then take her HOME. Thank you, Lord. Your will be done - your will be done – your will be done!"

Once again that gentle hand was on my shoulder. Tears were streaming down my face as I hugged my wife and told her I knew that, no matter what, all is well. We watched through the night. In the morning the doctors and nurses were more positive. A day or so later we left the hospital with our precious gift smiling once again.

She's a grandmother now. And the irony of it all, is that she bore us five grandsons (and little stillborn Michael) to add to her sister's four boys. God was telling me, *"Gus, you wanted a son. Now you have enough grandsons to field a baseball team."*

GREAT IS THY FAITHFULNESS, O LORD!

Lamentations 3:23

AT 65

January 8, 2004

It's my birthday. A significant milestone.

In 1949 I was ten years old. I wondered if I would live to see the year 2000. (Three years of the new millennium have come and gone). Back then I was anxious to be a teen-ager. My sister was 15, and on her high school's volleyball team. That's what I wanted – to be a part of a team - basketball or football. I was stuck in those intervening years and I had to convince myself that BEING TEN WAS GOOD

What a relief it was to turn twenty and not be a teen-ager any longer. In only a year, at twenty one, I would be a full-fledged adult – or so I thought. In two and one-half years I would finish college and get married. I knew exactly what my life's vocation was going to be and I knew with whom I was going to share that life. BEING TWENTY WAS GOOD

At thirty, another decade had gone by. Many of my prayers had been answered. Margaret and I had three beautiful daughters. I had completed graduate work and had a position as a principal in a Lutheran school. Although we had just experienced two major crisis (our twenty-month old almost died in a Port Arthur hospital, and I had gone to M.D. Anderson in Houston, fearing the possibility of cancer), the

Lord proved His love and faithfulness in both instances. BE-
ING THIRTY WAS GOOD

By age forty life had taken a different direction – one
I never dreamed would have happened. I had resigned my
principal/teaching position and had to find employment elsewhere – not exactly sure where to turn. Thank God for a
loving brother-in-law who secured a place for me – just to
get us through, while I sought something in line with my
background and training. I was sure that I would not be with
White-Tucker Company for long. Life was challenging, and
yet... BEING FORTY WAS GOOD

On my fiftieth birthday I had been at White-Tucker
for over fourteen years, longer than I had spent in the teaching profession. Camille, our youngest, would soon be fin-
ishing college and Margaret and I would be "empty nesters."
Our other two daughters, Pam and Lori, were both married
and we had two grandchildren, both of them girls. It seemed
that I was destined to be son-less, except for sons-in-law.
But the blessing of "sons" was yet to come, and come in
abundance. BEING FIFTY WAS GOOD

I had a wonderful sixtieth birthday party, with all of
my children, their husbands and twelve, yes count them
T-W-E-L-V-E grandchildren, eight of them BOYS. I was
still employed at White-Tucker, and it was obvious that I
would continue there until retirement. Plans and hopes for a
change several years earlier didn't materialize. A big disappointment! I would have been good at that job at Compaq....and it was much closer to home...and the working

conditions were more attractive than the warehousing district where White-Tucker was...and the salary and benefits would have been better.... and...and...and I stayed with White-Tucker...and the Lord knew what He was doing. In less than a year Compaq was sold and the position I sought disappeared. BEING SIXTY WAS GOOD

I looked into the mirror this morning and a sixty-five year old man stared back. When you are young – ten, twenty, even thirty or forty – people sixty-five are "old folks." You know that one day you will, more than likely, get there. But age creeps up on you so gradually and yet so swiftly, that it's here before you know it. Oh, preparations have been made – signing up for Social Security and Medicare and informing White-Tucker of tentative retirement plans – another year down the road. However, today I am officially OLD. I can now accept those store and restaurant discounts without reservation or twinges of guilt or pangs of vanity. Today I am an "honest-to-goodness senior citizen."

But I don't feel old, except when getting up off the floor while playing with my grandchildren. My health is strong; my mind is alert (at least I hope this narrative makes sense). But, what has happened to all of the years? What about those dreams that never came true?

The years have been wonderful! I now have fifteen grandchildren, including enough boys to field a baseball team, and awaiting another grandchild in April. Granddaughters: don't misunderstand – you each are as precious to me as any of the boys – it's just that I have been surrounded by females for so long, the fact that I now have nine grandsons just proves God's generosity and, I believe, His wonderful sense of humor. He wanted to show me that He could give what He had previously withheld, and give it to overflowing.

And those dreams that never came true – those of my youth, were likely unrealistic in the first place. Those of a young adult that were never realized…well, it's an adage that may be overused, but nevertheless has been true for me: "When God closes a door, He always opens a window." The disappointments were turned into blessings – on top of all the other blessings in my life. Try as I may, it is impossible to list them all. I trust that each of you knows and loves the Lord as much as you say you do. Without Him, life is a meaningless disaster. It is hard to imagine that the joy of heaven will be complete if even one of you is missing.

And what would life be without you, Margaret? Without you?… my love - my joy……………………………… …………………………………………………………..…empty.

I thank God that you are beside me still. What days or years we have left to share, whatever the circumstances, you will be, as you have always been, my greatest and most cherished earthly blessing. Every additional day with you is a blessed day that I do not deserve. BEING SIXTY-FIVE IS GOOD

Oh give thanks unto the Lord,

For He is good

And His mercies endure forever!

Psalm 106:1

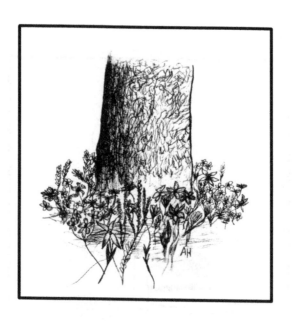

GRIEF AND JOY

ON RETURNING FROM LAYING TO REST THE TINY,
DELICATE REMAINS OF

MY GRANDSON, MATTHEW MICHAEL HARRIS, BORN
PREMATURE AND LIFELESS THIS MORNING

JUNE 13, 1998

It is difficult to begin writing what I now feel. (I have already been interrupted twice by tears, and I have no idea how far I will be able to go.) My mind is all cluttered...but I want to attempt to put into words what my heart yearns to say.

Yesterday, we heard Camille's visit to the doctor was heartbreaking. No life could be detected. It hurt, deeply, because we knew that she loves this child – already so precious, as all of her children are. Then, today we learned the doctor's assessment was true...Camille delivered the lifeless, yet recognizable, body of the son she and Glen named MATTHEW MICHAEL.

As I drove to their home alone (Margaret had gone ahead) a real sense of joy filled my heart as I marveled at how gracious God was to this little boy – to spare him all of the woes and heartaches that we must endure here on earth. We pray "Come Lord Jesus," (Revelation 22:20) and yet HE tarries. For Matthew Michael that prayer was answered before he could utter a sound. Now he sings and shouts in eternal joy. I feel "cheated." Heaven is his so soon.

217

The tears came once again.

Mixed with the joy is sadness – selfish sadness, I know – for the times I will never spend with this grandson – times that give me such happiness, like those I have with the rest of my grandchildren. Matthew Michael, I will not know those times with you. And I grieve – for the hours I will not have to share "grandpa things" – like showing you how to mow the lawn and trim everything in the corners or gazing at the planets and stars - Orion and The Pleiades…but then, you already know more of the galaxies than I shall ever see here – glories no one on earth has ever witnessed. Oh, how I envy you, Matthew Michael!

He was so tiny – only 18 weeks – I hesitated to even look at him at first. But I know for sure that the child I beheld may have been "premature" as the world considers things… but in God's eyes Matthew Michael was exactly what HE wanted him to be…complete…and the Lord called him…HOME.

We returned the little body to the dust from which it came – in the shade of an oak tree beside the house. With saddened boldness Glen led us in praising God for HIS goodness, HIS faithfulness, and HIS love. We fed on God's Word (Psalm 139) and as Glen led us in prayer and song I silently thanked God once again for the Christian husband and father He gave to Camille and their boys.

The grief is gone - joy has returned.

but

There will still be tears.

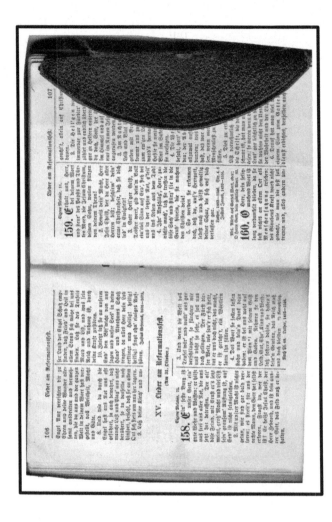

MY FATHER'S HYMNAL

The photo of my father's *Kirchengesangbuch* (Church song book) is opened to one of his favorite hymns, *Ein Feste Burg (A Mighty Fortress).* He more than likely received it as a confirmation gift when he was thirteen or fourteen years old (1918 or 1919). In those days the members of Zion Lutheran Church brought their own hymnals or sang from memory.

The book is small in comparison to most hymnals today. When opened, its actual size measures a mere five by seven inches. The text in the Old Germanic alphabet is incredibly small with each column of print slightly over an inch wide. Therefore, sharing with one's neighbor in the pew was next to impossible. Although a book of songs, every verse appears in paragraph form, rather than rhyming poetic lines. There are no musical notations, but following the organ accompaniment, many in the congregation would harmonize their familiar hymns.

Its front leather cover, with GUS F JACOB embossed in gold, has disappeared, but the gilded edges, though dulled by wear, remain, along with the back cover and the arched closure flap. In spite of the ancient script, I can still decipher and translate a few of the words and phrases, but I fear that my old German professor would hide his face in shame - I left his tutorage with no satisfying command of the 'mother tongue' he loved.

I NEVER HEARD MY FATHER SING

There was always music in our home – the piano or that old Crosley radio atop the refrigerator playing on most of the day. On Saturday evenings, as Vangie and I washed dishes, the stars of "Your Hit Parade" sang the top tunes of the week. (That's when our parents usually left the room.) And it wasn't just music from the piano or the radio – there was music from Momma – humming or singing as she cooked and ironed and sewed or rocked baby sister in her lap.

Momma was the 'musician' in the family. As far back as I can remember, our upright piano sat in the same corner of our living room. I believe it was Momma's even before she and Daddy were married. As kids, there were evenings when Vangie and I would sit on the piano bench at either side of Momma as she played, and the three of us sang together. Daddy would relax in an overstuffed chair nearby, reading his *Ft .Worth Star Telegram* or *Wall Street Journal*, but he was listening too.

Once, around the age of nine or ten, I found the splintered scrolled neck of an old violin in the attic. I asked Momma about it and all she said was, "That's something your daddy bought years ago. He thought he would learn to play, but…(sigh)... he never did." I couldn't imagine Daddy with a fiddle under his chin. I knew better than to ask him to explain.

My father loved music – although I never saw him touch the piano keyboard or hold a single instrument in his hand. If some choir or musical touring group was scheduled to perform in town or at church, we were there. I recall that once, following a concert by an instrumental trio, Daddy purchased a stack of their recordings. Why? I couldn't imagine – we never owned a phonograph to play them on.

The strong, sweet voices of the Bamch sisters always sounded forth from the fifth bench on the right side of Zion's nave. Daddy's favorite spot was directly in front of the young ladies. He would turn up his hearing-aid, open his personal leather-bound hymnal and silently follow along. As the congregation sang he attended each line. Deep inside, his heart was singing. I don't know why he never joined in. Perhaps it was occasioned by his hearing loss, or he thought he was one not blessed with a voice for singing.

I can remember the sound of Daddy's voice – the sound of him scolding me for something I'd done or left undone – the sound of him bantering with customers in the store – his lively 'discussions' with uncles on Sunday afternoons at Grandma's. But the most vivid recollection is his reading the Bible at our family devotions each day and the sound of his voice in prayer. Sadly, however, there is a sound I wish I could recall but never will, because…

…I never heard my father sing.

ACKNOWLEDGEMENTS

Hats off to all who encouraged me to undertake this project, especially my daughters, Pamela, Lorraine and Camille. Your input and critique were invaluable.

To my grandchildren Noah, Abigail, Zachary, and Arleah for your sketches, and Malachi for the front cover photography - all beautiful - thank you all so much.

To "granddaughters-in-law" Bridget and Gabby for additional sketches, proofreading and corrections - you are so appreciated.

To my siblings, Vangie, Arlene and John - I am indebted to you for your input - topical suggestions, corrections in matters of fact and overall support.

To Margaret, my beloved, I thank God for you - for loving me all these years and especially for understanding and forgiving the countless hours I labored at the computer keys. I love you.

APPENDIX

Jacob's Store - c 1940

Andice School - now Andice Community Center

ANDICE - c 1935 - Looking north to the "T" intersection

Zion Lutheran Church - Walburg Texas- c 1950

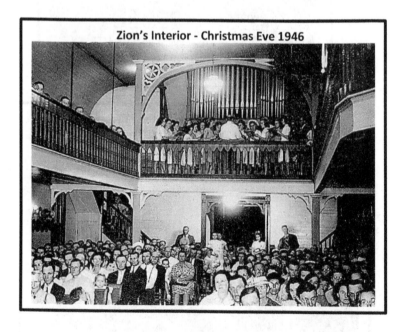

Zion's Interior - Christmas Eve 1946

July 9, 1961

Margaret and our daughters - 2020
L-R: Pamela, Margaret, Lorraine, Camille

Siblings - 1997
L-R: Evangeline (Vangie), Gus, Arlene, John

School Rhythm Band - sister Arlene center row 2nd from right

GRANDMOTHER KELM'S PEACH PIE

Pre-heat oven to 325 degrees
Prepare peach mixture and custard in separate containers
Nine or ten 2 ½" diameter peaches (3 lbs.) should yield 4 cups of sliced peaches

PIE FILLING (for 9 ½" pie plate)	PIE FILLING (for 9" pie plate)
4 cups peach pieces (bite size)	3 cups peach pieces
1/3 cup dark brown sugar, packed	¼ cup drk brown sugar
1/3 cup granulated sugar	¼ cup granulated sugar
½ teaspoon salt	½ teaspoon salt
1 Tablespoon lemon juice	1 Tablespoon lemon juice
1 teaspoon cinnamon	¾ teaspoon cinnamon
2 rounded Tablespoons corn starch	2 Tablespoons corn starch

1. Thoroughly mix sugars, cinnamon, salt and corn starch in medium sized bowl. Approximately 5 minutes before pouring into unbaked pie shell, stir together peaches with sugar mixture, allowing juice to develop.
2. Pour peach mixture into unbaked pie shell, approximately ¾ full,
3. Drizzle custard mixture over peaches. DO NOT STIR. Open peach mixture with a fork to allow custard to flow into peaches. Fill with custard until shell is almost completely full, leaving ½ " to top of crust to allow expansion of custard as it bakes.(Custard will shrink back when cooled). Continue baking until custard is done and set (custard's liquid sheen will be gone – toothpick inserted into center will come out clean) 55-60 minutes. (Rotate pie halfway thru the baking time)

***** ***** *****

CUSTARD (for 9 ½" deep dish pie plate)	CUSTARD (for 9" pie plate)
3 eggs	2 eggs
1/3 cup granulated sugar	¼ cup granulated sugar
3/4 cup heavy cream	½ cup heavy cream
1 teaspoon vanilla	1 teaspoon vanilla

Whisk eggs until blended; add remaining ingredients and whisk thoroughly. Allow mixture to come to room temperature or warm it slightly (but do not cook),   (Stir well before pouring it into the pie.)

GRANDMOTHER JACOB'S SMEARKÄSE

s(h)mear – käse [< German < schmieren = to spread or smear -
käse = cheese]
Generously spread this soft, mild cheese over fresh home-made bread
or on your favorite rye, pumpernickel or sour-dough bread – Great with
pretzel sticks and many snack crackers

INGREDIENTS
72 ounces regular large-curd cottage cheese (Do NOT use 2% or low
fat) - Yield: approx. 3 pints
1 ½ Tablespoons baking soda
 10 Tablespoons butter (1 ¼ sticks)
¾ teaspoon salt (omit salt if using salted butter)
1 cup heavy cream

1. DRY THE COTTAGE CHEESE: In a large colander rinse the milky
whey from the cottage cheese. Place a second colander with rinsed cottage cheese over a container to drain curds. Spread the curds on large
rimmed baking sheet to expose as many as possible to the air. Place
uncovered in the refrigerator for several hours, stirring and re-spreading
occasionally.
2. Melt the butter in large double boiler (Upper pan should be no more
than 2/3 full after all ingredients have been added)
Add the cheese curds, salt, soda and cream – heat slowly (med-low
heat) stirring CONTINUOUSLY and scraping bottom of pan until
curds are completely dissolved. Mixture will become "foamy" and
begin to rise in the pot. Take care to avoid boiling over.
3. When all curds are dissolved remove from heat and allow to cool.
As mixture cools it will settle to original volume. Pour into storage
containers - cool, cover and refrigerate. Can be frozen
Serve chilled or at room temperature if you prefer a softer spread.

VARIATIONS
As mixture cools and begins to thicken, stir in caraway seeds, finely
chopped dill weed, red pepper flakes, finely chopped jalapenos, minced
chives, or chopped herbs.

SWEET PICKLED WATERMELON RIND (yield: 2 quarts)
   This recipe requires refrigeration - not open-shelf-stable.
   Need: 2 clean wide-mouth quart jars with tight-fitting lids

BRINE (bring following to boil - reduce heat and simmer 5 min.)
2 cups water
2 cups cider vinegar
3 cups sugar
½ tsp black peppercorns
2 tsp coriander seeds
1 tsp celery seeds
2 bay leaves (one for each jar))
½ tsp red pepper flakes (optional or to taste) For HOT SWEET
      PICKLED RIND use 1 Tablespoon red pepper flakes
½ tsp whole cloves
1 cinnamon stick (broken in half – one half for each   of the two jars)
1 T kosher salt

WATERMELON PREPARATION:
After removing the red flesh for regular consumption, cut rind into ½
inch thick quarter-moon circles - trim the rind, leaving small amount of
red flesh (approx. ¼ inch)
With a sharp knife, remove and discard approx. 1/8 inch of the green
outer rind.
Cut remaining rind (white with red) into 1" slices or size you prefer
Add rind to simmering brine – bring to a boil – boil for 5-8 minutes
Fork test for desired tenderness – Boil additional time if desired
Place rind into the jars. Fill to within 1/2 "of top rim.
Pour the hot brine into each jar covering the rind. Try to divide spices
evenly between the jars.
Place the lids on tightly and set aside to cool completely
Invert the jars and cool in the refrigerator for 4 days, inverting the jars
every 24 hours to allow the brine to mix and the spices to circulate.
Keeps in refrigerator for 4-6 weeks.
Excellent served with barbeque pulled-pork or munch alone.

Made in the USA
Coppell, TX
06 December 2020